Collins

Student Support Materials for AQA

AS Biology

Unit 1: Biology and Disease

Author: Mike Boyle

Series Editors: Keith Hirst and Lesley Higginbottom

William Collins's dream of knowledge for all began with the publication of his first book in 1819. A self-educated mill worker, he not only enriched millions of lives, but also founded a flourishing publishing house. Today, staying true to this spirit, Collins books are packed with inspiration, innovation and practical expertise. They place you at the centre of a world of possibility and give you exactly what you need to explore it.

Collins. Freedom to teach.

Published by Collins
An imprint of HarperCollinsPublishers
77-85 Fulham Palace Road
Hammersmith
London
W6 8JB

Browse the complete Collins catalogue at
www.collinseducation.com

© HarperCollinsPublishers Limited 2008

10 9 8 7 6 5 4 3 2 1

ISBN-13 978-0-00-726817-7

Mike Boyle asserts his moral right to be identified as the author of this work.

British Library Cataloguing in Publication Data. A Catalogue record for this publication is available from the British Library.

Commissioned by Penny Fowler
Series Editors Keith Hirst and Lesley Higginbottom
Edited by Kath Senior
Proof read by Rachel Hutchings
Design by Newgen Imaging
Cover design by Angela English
Production by Arjen Jansen
Printed and bound in Hong Kong by Printing Express

Mixed Sources
Product group from well-managed forests and other controlled sources
www.fsc.org Cert no. SW-COC-1806
© 1996 Forest Stewardship Council

FSC is a non-profit international organisation established to promote the responsible management of the world's forests. Products carrying the FSC label are independently certified to assure consumers that they come from forests that are managed to meet the social, economic and ecological needs of present and future generations.

Find out more about HarperCollins and the environment at
www.harpercollins.co.uk/green

Contents

3.1.1   Disease may be caused by infectious pathogens or may reflect the effects of lifestyle.   4

3.1.2   The digestive system provides an interface with the environment. Digestion involves enzymic hydrolysis producing smaller molecules that can be absorbed and assimilated.   4

3.1.3   Substances are exchanged between organisms and their environment by passive or active transport across exchange surfaces. The structure of plasma membranes enables control of the passage of substances across exchange surfaces.   16

3.1.4   The lungs of a mammal also act as an interface with the environment. Lung function may be affected by pathogens and factors relating to lifestyle.   27

3.1.5   The functioning of the heart plays a central role in the circulation of blood and relates to the level of activity of an individual. Heart disease may be linked to factors affecting lifestyle.   30

3.1.6   Mammalian blood possesses a number of defensive functions.   35

How Science Works   41

Practice exam-style questions   50

Answers, explanations, hints and tips   56

Glossary   58

Index   66

Notes   70

3.1.1 Disease may be caused by infectious pathogens or may reflect the effects of lifestyle.

There are three types of disease: each one is defined by its cause:

1 **Infectious diseases** are the ones you can catch. These **communicable diseases** are caused by **pathogens**: bacteria, **viruses**, fungi or parasites.

2 **Lifestyle diseases** can't be caught. These are **non-communicable diseases** that are caused by environmental factors such as diet, smoking and pollution.

3 **Genetic diseases** include inherited conditions (mainly covered in Unit 2).

Some diseases have an obvious single cause, as Table 1 shows. Others, such as diabetes, Alzheimer's and most types of cancer are usually caused by a complex interaction of several factors. For example, a genetic tendency, triggered by an unhealthy lifestyle, or exposure to a particular virus, may lead to the onset of a disease.

Table 1
Some disease examples

Infectious diseases (pathogen)	Lifestyle diseases	Genetic diseases
AIDS (virus)	Coronary heart disease	Cystic fibrosis
Influenza (virus)	Some types of cancer	Sickle cell anaemia
Tuberculosis (bacterium)	Emphysema	Huntington's disease
Cholera (bacterium)		Haemophilia
Athlete's foot (fungus)		

Essential Notes

The word **interface** means 'point of connection'. The skin, lungs and intestines are all interfaces with the environment: all are possible routes by which pathogens can enter the body.

Examiners' Notes

Many exam questions contain data about risk factors and ask you to interpret them. You also need to be able to interpret data on correlations.

Once they are inside the body, pathogens avoid the host's immune system, get inside cells and start multiplying, causing disease symptoms in the process. Pathogens cause disease by damaging cells directly as they invade them and/or by the action of their **exotoxins**, secreted substances that interfere with the host's **metabolism** in some way. Some exotoxins cause mild symptoms, others can be lethal.

3.1.2 The digestive system provides an interface with the environment. Digestion involves enzymic hydrolysis producing smaller molecules that can be absorbed and assimilated.

This section is about what is in food and how we digest it. First, some basics:

- The food we eat contains plant and animal tissue, which contains lots of large, complex molecules locked inside cells.

- Food also contains some bacteria, which may or may not be harmful.

- In **digestion**, we must first break open the cells – cooking and chewing food both help. We then **hydrolyse** (break down) the large molecules until they are small enough to be absorbed into the blood.

- The main types of large organic molecules are **protein**, **carbohydrate** and **lipid**.
- Proteins are hydrolysed into **amino acids**.
- Carbohydrates are hydrolysed into **simple sugars**, mainly **glucose**.
- Lipids are hydrolysed into **fatty acids** and **glycerol**.
- These molecules, along with minerals, vitamins and water, are absorbed into the blood through the gut wall.
- Once inside the body the simple food molecules are **assimilated**; they are used to make cells and cell components, or broken down for energy.

Overview of the digestive system

The human gut is essentially a long, muscular tube that stretches from mouth to anus (Fig 1).

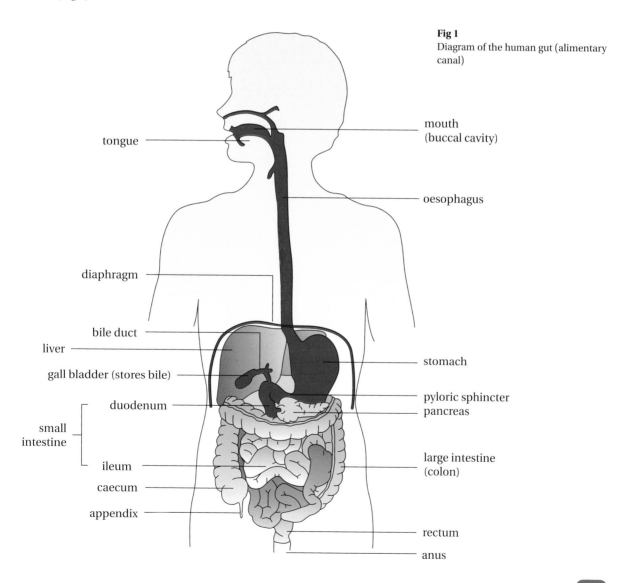

Fig 1
Diagram of the human gut (alimentary canal)

tongue

mouth (buccal cavity)

oesophagus

diaphragm

bile duct

liver

gall bladder (stores bile)

duodenum

small intestine

ileum

caecum

appendix

stomach

pyloric sphincter
pancreas

large intestine (colon)

rectum

anus

Various glands along the gut secrete digestive juices. There are four main digestive juices:

- **Saliva:** secreted by three pairs of salivary glands in the mouth.
- **Gastric juice**: made by the stomach lining.
- **Bile:** made by the liver.
- **Pancreatic juice**: produced by the pancreas.

These juices contain a variety of substances that control the digestive process. However, this unit focuses only on carbohydrate digestion, so you need to consider only saliva and pancreatic juice. You don't need to learn about gastric juice and bile.

Generally, these four main digestive juices begin digestion but the process is finished off by enzymes fixed in the membrane of the epithelial cells in the gut lining. Before we can look at enzymes, we need to look at proteins.

Proteins in detail

Proteins are very important in living things and the human body is no exception:

- Proteins called **enzymes** control metabolism (body chemistry) – there is a different enzyme for every reaction.
- **Antibodies** are proteins that are a vital part of the immune system and they help us to fight disease.
- **Actin** and **myosin** are proteins that bring about muscle contraction.
- **Collagen** gives strength to connective tissues. Tendons, cartilage and bone all owe their strength to collagen.
- Many different proteins are involved in **blood clotting**.
- **Keratin** is the protein that gives strength to hair, skin and nails.
- Proteins in cell membranes are vital in **cell transport** and **cell recognition**. Each human cell has a unique combination of proteins and other chemicals on its surface – this is why organ transplants are rejected unless careful matching is done.

A huge variety of different proteins perform all these functions. The function of an individual protein depends on its structure.

The structure of proteins

Proteins contain the elements carbon, hydrogen, oxygen and nitrogen. They often also contain sulphur and phosphorus.

Proteins are made up from sub-units called amino acids (Fig 2). There are 20 different amino acids. The fact that amino acids can be joined in any order to form an infinite number of different protein molecules is the key to why there is such a large variety of proteins.

Two amino acids join together in a **condensation** reaction to form a **dipeptide** (Fig 3). A chain of amino acids is known as a **polypeptide**. A protein may consist of one or more polypeptides.

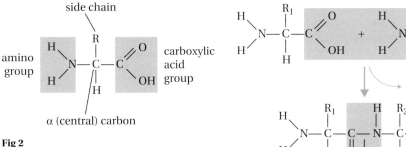

Fig 2
The basic structure of an amino acid. It's one of the basic molecules that you need to know

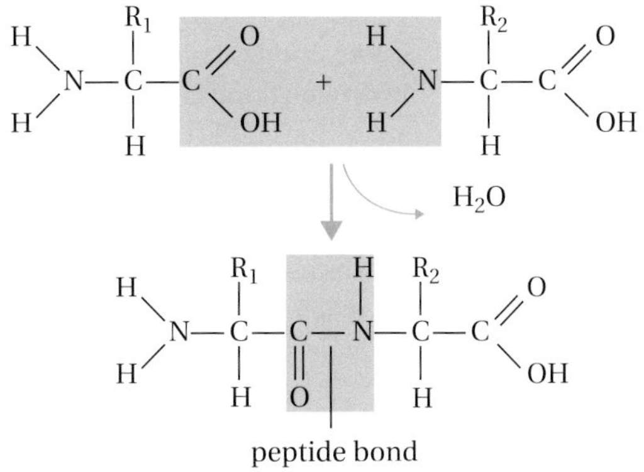

Essential Notes

As there are 20 different amino acids, there can be $20 \times 20 = 400$ different dipeptides. Proteins consist of hundreds, or even thousands, of amino acids, so the number of different ones is practically infinite. Put simply, there is a great variety of proteins because there are many different building blocks.

Proteins can be divided into two groups. **Globular proteins** such as enzymes, are roughly spherical, individual molecules that usually have a chemical function in organisms. In other words, they take part in a particular reaction. **Fibrous proteins**, which include collagen and keratin, have a structural role, such as giving strength or elasticity to a particular tissue.

The structure of proteins is complex and can be studied on four levels:

- primary
- secondary
- tertiary
- quaternary.

The **primary structure** is the sequence of amino acids in the polypeptide. An example would be alanine–glycine–leucine–valine–glutamic acid.

The **secondary structure** is the shape formed by the amino acid chain when the amino acids bend and twist to form the most stable arrangement. The commonest secondary structure is the **α helix** – a spiral shape. The **β pleated sheet** is another common secondary structure. Different regions of a polypeptide chain will have different forms of secondary structure within them (Fig 4).

Fig 3
The formation of a dipeptide from two amino acids by a condensation reaction. Amino acids always join in the same way: the amino group of one amino acid joins with the acid group of another ('nose to tail'). So, if there is an NH_2 group at one end of the chain, there will be a –COOH group at the other.

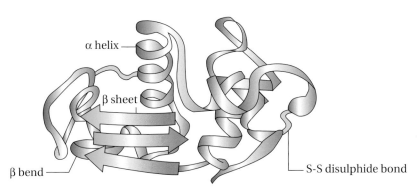

Fig 4
The tertiary structure of the protein lysozyme, an anti-bacterial compound that is present in secretions such as tears and sweat. The secondary structure is illustrated by showing α helices as spiral ribbons and β pleated sheets as broad flat arrows. You can see that there are different regions of secondary structure within the overall (tertiary) structure. Strong disulphide bonds help to maintain the shape.

The **tertiary structure** is the overall shape of the polypeptide chain (Fig 4). When a polypeptide chain bends or folds back on itself, weak bonds – commonly **hydrogen bonds** – form that stabilise the whole molecule. **Disulphide bridges** are strong bonds that can form between two sulphur-containing amino acids.

If the protein consists of only one polypeptide, the tertiary structure is the overall shape of the molecule. Some proteins consist of more than one polypeptide, in which case the **quaternary structure** is the shape created when the different polypeptide chains bind together to form the whole molecule. Insulin, for example, consists of two polypeptides; haemoglobin consists of four.

The shape of a globular protein is absolutely vital to its function. An enzyme, for instance, must have a precise tertiary and quaternary structure, otherwise it will not work. High temperature will make the molecule vibrate, breaking the weak bonds and changing the shape of the protein. This process is known as **denaturation** and it prevents the protein functioning properly. Extremes of pH can also cause denaturation.

Fig 5
The Biuret test for proteins. Add a few drops of Biuret solution (a light blue compound containing copper sulphate and sodium hydroxide) to the sample to be tested. If the sample contains protein the solution will turn *lilac* (pale purple). The reaction can be speeded up by heating gently. (Note: Biuret solution is corrosive.)

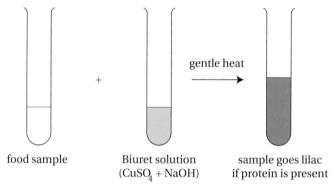

food sample

Biuret solution
($CuSO_4$ + NaOH)

gentle heat

sample goes lilac
if protein is present

Enzymes

Some important facts you need to remember about enzymes:

- Enzymes control the rate of all **metabolic reactions**. The term **metabolism** refers to the many inter-related chemical reactions that take place inside an organism. This is an incredibly complex system that must be controlled, so enzymes have a vital function.

- Enzymes are proteins. They are usually named by adding the suffix '-ase' to the name of the **substrate** and/or the type of reaction being catalysed. For example, alcohol dehydrogenase removes a hydrogen atom from alcohol; **sucrase** breaks down sucrose.

- Enzymes are **catalysts**. This means that they speed up reactions and are not used up by the reactions they catalyse.

A chemical reaction will not happen unless it has enough **activation energy**. In industrial processes, activation energy is often provided as heat but living organisms cannot create or survive very high temperatures. Enzymes speed up reactions by splitting up the reaction pathway into small steps that require less energy. This enables the overall reaction to take place more easily and at lower temperatures.

Essential Notes

Activation energy is the energy needed to break existing bonds before new bonds can form.

Each enzyme has a pocket or groove in the enzyme surface that is called the **active site**. This is the exact shape to match up precisely with the substrate (Fig 6). It should be obvious, therefore, that there can only be one enzyme for each reaction: enzymes are specific.

As the reaction starts, the substrate binds momentarily to the active site of the enzyme to form an **enzyme–substrate complex**. The substrate is then transformed into product. This model of enzyme action is the **lock and key hypothesis** – only one substrate (the key) will fit into the active site (the lock). It is now thought that the active site changes shape so that the enzyme moulds itself around the substrate: this modification of the lock and key idea is known as the **induced fit hypothesis**.

Examiners' Notes

The fact that enzymes are proteins is a key idea for examinations, so make sure that you are familiar with the biochemistry of proteins (pages 6–8).

(a)

Enzyme + substrate   Enzyme + substrate complex   Enzyme + products

Fig 6
(a) The lock and key hypothesis – the substrate and active site are complementary in terms of shape and chemical charges.

(b)

Active site moulds around substrate

Enzyme + substrate   Enzyme + substrate complex   Enzyme + products

(b) The induced fit hypothesis – as the substrate combines with the active site, the enzyme molecule alters its shape and moulds itself around the substrate.

Essential Notes

The **turnover number** is the number of substrate molecules turned into product per minute by one molecule of enzyme. It gives a measure of the speed of enzyme action. A typical value would be 200 000.

Examiners' Notes

DO NOT describe the active site and the substrate as the SAME SHAPE! They are COMPLEMENTARY.

Enzyme properties

The properties of enzymes reflect the fact that they are proteins. Enzymes have a precise but delicate tertiary structure. Anything that disrupts this structure (such as high temperature or pH) or that affects the rate of formation of the enzyme–substrate complex (for example, by blocking the active site) will interfere with enzyme activity.

Temperature

As temperature increases, so does the rate of reaction up to a critical temperature at which the enzyme becomes denatured (Fig 7). Increasing temperature gives molecules more kinetic energy, so there are more collisions. This means that more enzyme–substrate complexes form, so the rate of reaction increases. At higher temperatures, however, the enzyme molecule vibrates so much that the weak bonds maintaining the tertiary structure are broken, the shape of the molecule changes and the enzyme can no longer work. At this point the enzyme is said to be **denatured**. The temperature at which this happens varies from enzyme to enzyme, but typically it is between 50 and 60 °C.

Examiners' Notes

If you are given data for enzymes that are active at higher temperatures, believe the data and explain them in terms of some proteins having stronger tertiary/quaternary bonding.

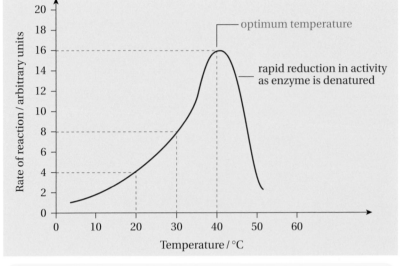

Fig 7
The relationship between enzyme activity and temperature

Essential Notes

The faster a substrate molecule moves the more likely it is to hit an active site.

Essential Notes

Thermophilic bacteria have **thermostable** enzymes that are not easily denatured. This enables them to survive at temperatures of up to 100 °C, for example, in hot volcanic springs or in deep ocean geothermal vents.

Examiners' Notes

In questions on substrate or enzyme concentration, the rate of reaction is shown by the gradient of the curve (steeper = faster reaction). When the graph levels off there must be another limiting factor.

pH

The formation of the enzyme–substrate complex depends on a precise match of shape and charge. If there is a change in pH, this can cause a change in the amount of free H^+ or OH^- ions, which can disrupt these charges. All enzymes have an optimum pH. Enzymes that work inside cells (intracellular) usually work best at a pH of 7.3–7.45 (Fig 8). Some extracellular enzymes, such as the digestive enzymes of the stomach and small intestine, work best at extremes of pH.

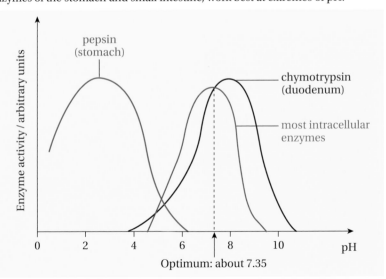

Fig 8
Graph showing the effect of pH on enzyme activity

Substrate concentration

The greater the substrate concentration, the faster the rate of reaction until the enzymes are working as fast as possible. This happens when *all* active sites are filled *all* the time (Fig 9). At this point the rate of reaction can only be increased further by adding more enzyme.

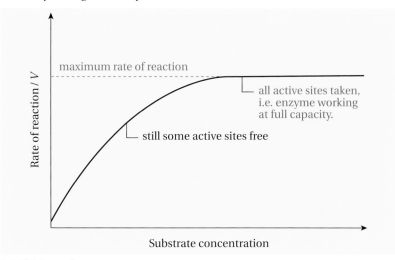

Examiners' Notes

In exam answers, always try to use A-level language. In enzyme questions, examiners expect to see words such as *collisions*, *enzyme–substrate complexes*, *tertiary structure*, *active site* and *denatured*.

Examiners' Notes

Be careful *not* to refer to an enzyme's active site as being 'used up'.

Fig 9
The relationship between substrate concentration and rate of reaction

Inhibition of enzymes

An **inhibitor** is a substance that slows down or stops enzyme action (Fig 10). Most reactions with inhibitors are **reversible**, which means that they do not combine with the enzyme molecule permanently. There are two types of reversible inhibitor, **competitive inhibitors** and **non-competitive inhibitors**.

Competitive inhibitors are very similar to the substrate in terms of their 3D shape. This allows them to enter the active site and effectively 'get in the way' so that the substrate cannot enter (Fig 11). They compete with the substrate for the active site. If more substrate is added, the effect of the inhibitor will be reduced.

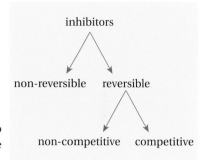

Fig 10
Simple overview of inhibition

Fig 11
The effect of a competitive inhibitor on enzyme activity

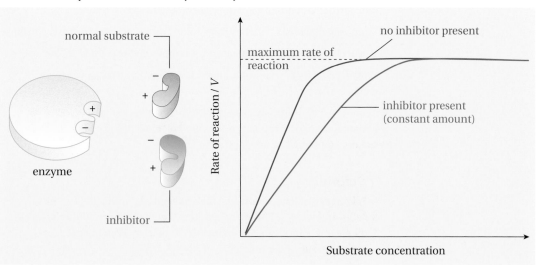

Non-competitive inhibitors bind to the enzyme molecule at a position away from the active site, but they change the tertiary structure. This modifies the shape of the active site so that the enzyme–substrate complex cannot form. In this case adding more substrate will have no effect on the rate of reaction, or on the level of inhibition (Fig 12).

Fig 12
The effect of a non-competitive inhibitor on enzyme activity

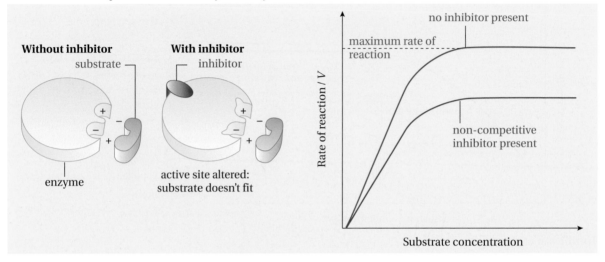

Essential Notes

Metabolism in living cells is largely controlled by non-competitive inhibitors that temporarily deactivate enzymes when their product is not needed. As a general idea, hormones work by switching enzymes and enzyme systems on or off. Think of enzymes as workers and hormones as bosses.

Carbohydrates and their digestion

Carbohydrates include **sugars**, **starches**, **cellulose** and **glycogen**. Carbohydrates always contain the elements carbon, hydrogen and oxygen, and can be divided into three categories according to size:

- **Monosaccharides** – 'single sugars', for example, glucose, fructose, galactose.

- **Disaccharides** – 'double sugars', for example, sucrose, maltose, lactose.

- **Polysaccharides** – 'multiple sugars', for example, starch, glycogen and cellulose.

Both mono- and disaccharides are classed as sugars and are sweet, white, water-soluble solids. Polysaccharides are polymers of sugars and are neither sweet nor soluble. They are covered in Unit 2.

Definition

Polymers are long, chain-like molecules made from simpler units called monomers. The carbohydrates starch, glycogen and cellulose are all polymers in which the monomer is glucose. Proteins are also polymers but lipids are not.

Monosaccharides

The commonest monosaccharide is glucose, which exists in two forms: **α glucose** and **β glucose** (Fig 13). The different forms affect the properties of the polymers that contain glucose (see **Glycogen and cellulose** sub-section, Unit 2).

Fig 14 shows how two glucose molecules join. They link by a condensation reaction that produces the disaccharide maltose along with one molecule of water. The two monosaccharides are linked by a **glycosidic bond** (C—O—C), where the molecules share an oxygen atom.

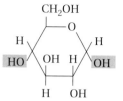

Fig 13
The basic structure of glucose. This is α glucose because both of the side –OH groups shown are pointing the same way. In β glucose one –OH points up, the other down. β glucose is covered in Unit 2.

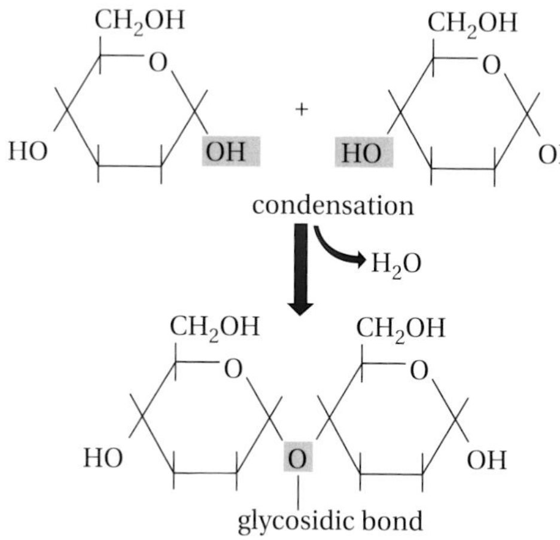

Fig 14
Two glucose molecules join to form the disaccharide maltose when a condensation reaction produces a glycosidic bond. (Note: the glucose molecules are simplified and some atoms are not shown.)

Examiners' Notes
Practise drawing the formation of maltose from two glucose molecules, and make sure you can label the glycosidic bond.

Disaccharides

Common examples of disaccharides, or 'double sugars', are maltose, sucrose and lactose:

- **Maltose** is formed from two glucose molecules. It is common in germinating seeds, where it is produced by the breakdown of starch.

- **Sucrose** is formed from a glucose and a fructose molecule. It is the main transport carbohydrate in plants, so is found in high concentration in phloem tissue.

- **Lactose** is formed from a glucose and a galactose. It is found in the milk of virtually all mammals.

Essential Notes
Remember that amylases remove disaccharides from the end of polysaccharide chains. This is why starch is hydrolysed to maltose.

Polysaccharides

There are three key polysaccharides, starch, glycogen and cellulose. Only starch is covered in this module. All three are polymers, formed from hundreds or thousands of glucose units.

Starch is the main storage compound in plants. Storage compounds need to be insoluble, compact and easily converted to energy. Starch is actually a mixture of two compounds, amylose and amylopectin (Fig 15). **Amylose** consists of single, unbranched chains of α glucose that form a spiral. **Amylopectin** consists of branched chains of α glucose molecules.

Examiners' Notes
Remember that storage molecules should ideally be large and insoluble so they do not have an osmotic effect and so that they are not able to diffuse out of storage cells.

Amylose and amylopectin are large molecules, which means that they are insoluble in water. They do not, therefore, have an osmotic effect (cause movement of water) in starch-containing cells. The spiral/branched structure of the molecules makes them very compact. The glucose in these compounds can only be released from the ends of the chain. As amylopectin has many branches, glucose can be released more quickly from this polysaccharide than from amylose. This is a classic example of relating structure to function.

Fig 15
Starch is a mixture of two compounds, amylose and amylopectin

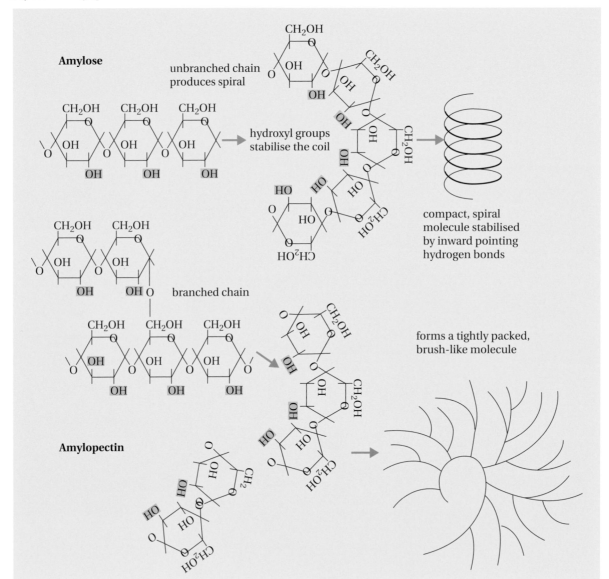

Carbohydrate digestion

Polysaccharides and disaccharides must be digested to monosaccharides before they can be absorbed.

Carbohydrate digestion begins in the mouth when the **amylase** enzyme in saliva begins to hydrolyse starch into maltose. This is only partial breakdown at best, because food doesn't stay in the mouth for long, and hot food can denature the enzyme. The acidic conditions in the stomach also deactivate salivary amylase.

There is no significant carbohydrate digestion in the stomach. Most carbohydrate digestion takes place in the duodenum. First, pancreatic amylase hydrolyses starch into maltose. Then carbohydrate digestion is completed by enzymes fixed in the membranes of the epithelial cells. The folded membrane in the epithelium is known as a brush border, and the three vital **brush border hydrolase enzymes** are maltase, lactase and sucrase:

- Maltase hydrolyses maltose into two molecules of glucose.
- Lactase hydrolyses lactose into a glucose and a galactose.
- Sucrase hydrolyses sucrose into a glucose and a fructose.

Lactose intolerance

This genetic condition occurs when an individual cannot make the enzyme lactase and so can't digest lactose – the main sugar in milk. Undigested lactose is used by gut bacteria. The result is abdominal bloating, pain, diarrhoea and wind. Many people are lactose intolerant, as are some animals. It has been estimated that over half of the world's population may be lactose intolerant.

Biochemical tests for carbohydrates

There are several simple biochemical tests that can be used to test for the presence of different carbohydrates.

Test for a reducing sugar

Add Benedict's solution to the compound to be tested. (Note: Benedict's solution is toxic.) Heat the mixture to near boiling point in a water bath. If the compound is a reducing sugar it will reduce the *blue* copper sulphate in the Benedict's solution into *orange* copper oxide which forms a precipitate (Fig 16).

Small amounts of reducing sugar will turn the mixture green and, generally, the higher the concentration of reducing sugar, the deeper the orange colour. This fact can be used to make a **quantitative** test – in other words, one that you can use to find out *how much* reducing sugar is contained in a particular sample. The amount of orange copper oxide can be compared either by filtering, drying and weighing the precipitate, or by using a **colorimeter** to estimate the depth of the orange colour (you have to compare the colour of your sample against a range of reference standards).

All the common monosaccharides (glucose, fructose and galactose) are reducing sugars, as are the disaccharides maltose and lactose. Note that sucrose is a non-reducing sugar.

Test for a non-reducing sugar

Non-reducing sugars (such as sucrose) can be detected by first boiling a sample that has previously tested negative for reducing sugar with dilute hydrochloric acid, then neutralising with sodium hydrogencarbonate. The acid hydrolyses the sugar to reducing sugars which will produce a positive result when the mixture is tested as above.

Test for starch

Add a small amount of *yellow/brown* iodine/potassium iodide solution to the compound to be tested. If starch is present a *blue/black* colour will be

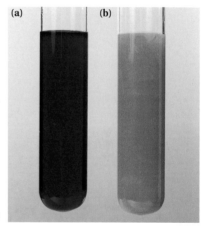

Fig 16 a and b
(a) Negative result for a reducing sugar
(b) Positive result for a reducing sugar

produced (Fig 16b). This is because the iodine fits into the spirals of the starch molecule to form a dark-coloured starch/iodine complex.

3.1.3 Substances are exchanged between organisms and their environment by passive or active transport across exchange surfaces. The structure of plasma membranes enables control of the passage of substances across exchange surfaces.

This section is about cells, membranes and how substances get across membranes to pass in or out of cells.

Typical animal cell

A good example of a typical animal cell is the epithelial cell from the small intestine (Fig 17). It is part of a tissue that lines the intestine and is adapted for the absorption of digested food. Under the light microscope these visible features are typical of most animal cells:

- The **nucleus** – a large circular structure that contains DNA.

- The **cell membrane** – a very thin membrane that surrounds the cell.

- The **cytoplasm** – literally 'cell fluid'. This contains many different structures, or **organelles** (see Fig 17).

See Table 2 on pages 18 and 19 for details about cell function.

Examiners' Notes

There is often a **light micrograph** and/or an **electron micrograph** to interpret on the exam paper – so make sure you can identify organelles in each.

Fig 17
The epithelial cells that line the small intestine show many typical features of animal cells

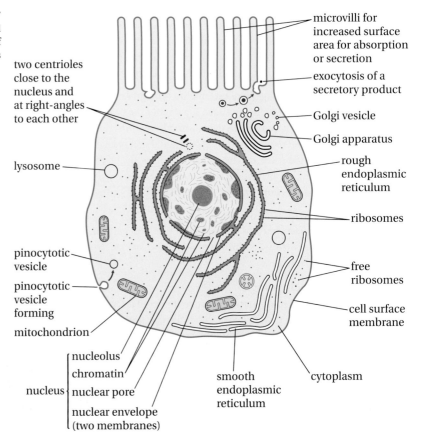

microvilli for increased surface area for absorption or secretion

two centrioles close to the nucleus and at right-angles to each other

exocytosis of a secretory product

Golgi vesicle

Golgi apparatus

lysosome

rough endoplasmic reticulum

ribosomes

pinocytotic vesicle

free ribosomes

pinocytotic vesicle forming

mitochondrion

cell surface membrane

nucleolus
chromatin
nucleus { nuclear pore
nuclear envelope (two membranes)

smooth endoplasmic reticulum

cytoplasm

Size and scaling

One millimetre is 1000 μm (**micrometres** or just microns) – cells and larger organelles that can generally be seen with a light microscope are measured in μm.

1 μm is 1000 nm (**nanometres**) – small organelles, such as ribosomes, and individual molecules are measured in nanometres. You need an electron microscope to see objects this small.

To work out the actual size of something in a photograph or diagram, you first measure it on the diagram and then use the magnification to work out its real size. For example, if the magnification was ×5000, each millimetre on the diagram would represent 1 five-thousandth of a millimetre in reality, which is 0.2 μm or 200 nm. If a mitochondrion measured 25 mm in the photograph, the actual size of the mitochondrion would be 0.2 × 25, which is 5 μm.

You may find the following triangle useful:

I = Image size on paper
M = Magnification
A = Actual size

Ultrastructure in eukaryotic cells

Ultrastructure means 'fine detail'. When viewed with an electron microscope, the cytoplasm of a plant or animal cell (called **eukaryotic** cells) is seen to contain many different organelles. The main ones are described in Table 2 (overleaf).

Cell fractionation

Individual organelles are easier to study when isolated from the rest of the cell. This can be done using **cell fractionation** and **ultracentrifugation**:

1 Tissue, such as liver, is chopped up and then **homogenised** (broken up to rupture the cells) using a 'blender'. Because this presents the opportunity for substances normally kept separate by cell membranes to mix together and react (such as digestive enzymes and their subtrates), this is all done in an ice cold **isotonic buffer solution** which:

- minimises enzyme reactions (low temperature)
- avoids distortion of organelles by water loss or gain
- resists any changes in pH that could be destructive.

2 The mixture is filtered to remove debris and then spun in an ultracentrifuge at high speed. The spinning greatly increases the gravitational field, and the organelles separate out according to density and, to some extent, shape.

3 First to separate out are the nuclei. The remaining fluid, the **supernatant** is poured off and centrifuged again to collect other organelles.

4 These are released in order of: mitochondria and lysosomes, rough ER, the plasma membranes and smooth ER and, finally, free ribosomes.

Examiners' Notes

$1\,mm = 10^{-3}\,m$. $1\,\mu m = 10^{-6}\,m$ and $1\,nm = 10^{-9}\,m$. Think, a nanometre is a thousandth of a thousandth of a thousandth of a metre. That's small.

Examiners' Notes

You must be able to work out the actual size of a cell or organelle when given the scale. Practise scaling calculations before examinations, and be familiar with the normal size of organelles so that you can recognise a silly answer when you see one.

Essential Notes

Isotonic means 'of the same water potential'. In this case, the fluid used has the same water potential as cell cytoplasm.

Definition

Water potential is a measure of the tendency of a solution cell to absorb water by osmosis.

Table 2
The main eukaryotic organelles

Organelle	Diagram	Description	Size/Distribution	Function
Plasma membrane, also called cell surface membrane		Thin boundary between cell and environment	Universal – it surrounds all cells in all organisms. Most organelles are surrounded by a similar membrane	Controls what passes in and out of the cell (see page 19). Similar membranes surround organelles, for example, mitochondria, nucleus. Proteins attached to the cell membrane play a part in cell recognition, for example, by the immune system and cell transport. **Microvilli** are folds in the membrane that increase the surface area for absorption.
Nucleus	nucleolus	Large, usually spherical, bounded by a double membrane with many pores	About 10 µm in diameter, usually one per cell	Contains the DNA. Key functions are replication, cell division and protein synthesis. In eukaryotic cells DNA is linear and attached to proteins (**histones**)
Mitochondrion		Usually round and elongated, smooth outer membrane, folded inner membrane	1–10 µm in size, up to 1000 in cytoplasm of each cell	Site of aerobic respiration – most of the cell's ATP is made here. The more metabolically active the cell, the more folds (**cristae**) there are in the mitochondria
Rough endoplasmic reticulum (rough ER)		Extensive membrane system, many cavities and tubes, ribosomes attached	Throughout cytoplasm, connected to nuclear membrane	Transport system in the cytoplasm; collects, stores, packages and transports the proteins made on the ribosomes
Smooth endoplasmic reticulum (smooth ER)		Membrane system with small cavities, no ribosomes attached	Small patches in cytoplasm	Synthesis of lipids and some steroids. Detoxification, for example, alcohol breakdown

Table 2 (*continued*)
The main eukaryotic organelles

Organelle	Diagram	Description	Size/Distribution	Function
Golgi apparatus		Stack of flattened membrane discs	Size varies, found free in cytoplasm close to rough ER	Receives packages (**vesicles**) of protein from rough ER. Appears to synthesise/ modify chemicals before their secretion from cell
Ribosome	small subunit — large subunit	Small and dense structure, like a giant enzyme. No membrane	Size 20 nm, attached to ER or free in cytoplasm	Site of translation: the part of the cell where the genetic code is used to build protein
Lysosome		Small vesicle (sphere) of membrane that contains digestive enzymes	Free in cytoplasm	Breakdown of substances, organelles or whole cells, for example, in phagocytosis, lysosomes are used by white cells to destroy bacteria

Cell membranes

This section is about cell membranes and how they work. First, we look at the structure and properties of **lipids**, then at the **phospholipids**, which make up cell membranes. Finally, we look at the overall structure of the membrane and the sections that follow consider its function.

Lipids

Lipids are a group of compounds that includes fats, oils and waxes. They all contain the elements carbon, hydrogen and oxygen. Importantly, *lipids don't mix with water*. You need to know about two types of lipid: **triglycerides** (which store energy) and phospholipids (which form membranes).

Triglycerides are commonly known as fats and oils. Triglyceride molecules are made from one molecule of glycerol (Fig 18) linked to three fatty acids. Fatty acids are **organic acids** (also called **carboxylic acids**) and always have a –COOH group. This group combines with an –OH group of a glycerol molecule during a condensation reaction. Each reaction forms an **ester bond** which, like the glycosidic bond, centres around a shared oxygen atom.

The hydrocarbon chain of a fatty acid contains between four and 22 carbon atoms. The fatty acids shown in Figs 19 and 20 are all **saturated**, which means they are saturated with hydrogen. **Unsaturated** fatty acids may have one C=C bond that can react with hydrogen to make saturated fatty acids. **Polyunsaturated** fatty acids have more than one C=C bond. Lipids that contain saturated fatty acids are usually solid at room temperature (fats), and those containing unsaturated fatty acids are usually liquid (oils).

> **Examiners' Notes**
>
> Polymers consist of repeated units (monomers) joined to each other. Lipids are not polymers.

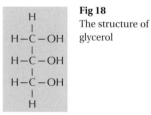

Fig 18
The structure of glycerol

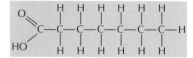

Fig 19
The structure of a short chain fatty acid

> **Examiners' Notes**
>
> Remember that fatty acids really are acidic and will therefore cause a lowering in pH when they are released during digestion (hydrolysis).

Fig 20
Three fatty acids combine
with glycerol to form a
triglyceride. Note the
ester bonds

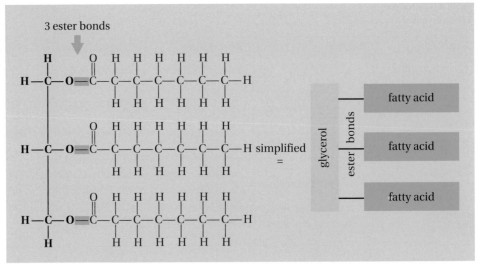

Triglycerides store energy: they can be respired to release more than twice as much energy as an equivalent mass of carbohydrate or protein. Other functions include insulation from the cold (for example, blubber in aquatic mammals) and protection of vital organs (for example, kidneys) from physical damage.

Lipids do not dissolve in water but they will dissolve in solvents such as **ethanol**. The **emulsion test** for lipids consists of adding ethanol to the sample and shaking it so that the lipid dissolves. The mixture is then poured into water. If the original sample contained lipid, a white emulsion (a suspension of fine droplets, like milk) will be produced.

Phospholipids

Phospholipids are vital in biology because they form membranes, such as the cell membrane (Fig 21). A phospholipid molecule is similar to a triglyceride except that one fatty acid is replaced by a phosphate group.

The phosphate group is highly **polar** (it carries a charge) and so attracts water molecules: in other words, it is **hydrophilic**. The fatty acid chains are not polar and so repel water, in other words, they are **hydrophobic**. So, in water, phospholipid molecules arrange themselves into structures such as micelles (spheres) and double layers (as in membranes), the hydrophilic parts pointing outwards and the hydrophobic tails pointing inwards. This automatic formation of membranes was essential to the evolution of life because it meant that the conditions inside a cell could be different to those outside.

Examiners' Notes

Practise drawing the structure of fatty acids and glycerol, and the way they combine to make a triglyceride. Make sure you can label the ester bonds, and don't forget that three water molecules are made in the process.

Fig 21
The structure of a phospholipid. The structure can be simplified into a sphere with two tails (often used in cell membrane diagrams)

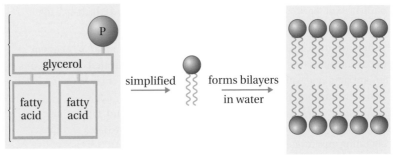

The structure of the cell membrane

The basic structure of the **plasma membrane**, or **cell membrane** (Fig 22) is described by the **fluid mosaic model**: 'mosaic' because there are many proteins in the membrane dotted around in a mosaic pattern, and 'fluid' because the pattern of proteins is continually changing. The membrane has very little physical strength at all, it's very thin (about 8 nm), but it does have a vital part to play in the control of what enters and leaves the cell.

The plasma membrane is made up of a phospholipid bilayer and proteins. The **phospholipid bilayer** forms a barrier to water-soluble substances such as sugars, amino acids and ions (for example, Na^+, Cl^-). Water itself can pass through the

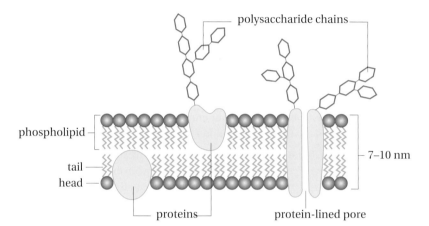

Fig 22
'Protein icebergs in a lipid sea' is one way to describe the fluid mosaic model of the plasma membrane

membrane with relative ease. Lipid-soluble substances, such as vitamins A, D, E and K, can pass freely across the membrane, as can the gases oxygen and carbon dioxide.

The proteins embedded in cell membranes have a variety of functions:

- They act as hydrophilic pores through which water-soluble chemicals can pass. However, large water-soluble compounds, such as large proteins, may be too big to pass through the pores and so may be unable to enter the cell at all.

- They are sites of **active transport** and **facilitated diffusion** (see below).

- They form **specific receptor sites** for hormones and other substances, which means that hormones can have an effect on some cells and not others.

Movement in and out of cells

There are four basic processes by which individual molecules or ions can pass through membranes:

- diffusion

- facilitated diffusion

- osmosis

- active transport.

Larger volumes of liquid or solid can also pass into the cell by **endocytosis** or out of the cell by **exocytosis** (see page 36).

Diffusion

Diffusion is a simple idea; particles spread out. Gases and liquids can diffuse, but solids cannot. If a substance is in higher concentration in one place compared to another, the particles will move around randomly until they become evenly spread. That's diffusion.

> ### Definition
> **Diffusion** is the movement of particles from a region of relatively high concentration to a region of lower concentration until evenly spread.

Diffusion is a **passive** process – substances will move down a concentration gradient without any input of energy in the form of ATP from the cell. The rate of diffusion depends on:

- the difference in concentration, i.e. the concentration gradient
- the distance over which diffusion occurs
- the surface area between the two regions
- the temperature. The higher the temperature, the more kinetic energy the particles possess, so they move around faster and diffuse faster.

In order to increase the rate of diffusion, organisms must maximise surface area and concentration difference, and minimise the distance between the two areas. Organs that are adapted for exchange processes, such as the lungs and gills, illustrate this idea. They all have a large surface area, good blood supply (to maintain the concentration difference) and thin membranes.

Essential Notes

Remember, if you see the word *diffusion*, that net movement of molecules is always **down**, or *along* the concentration gradient, from high to low.

Facilitated diffusion

Diffusion is said to be **facilitated diffusion** when it is speeded up by specific proteins in cell membranes. These proteins pass substances across the membrane faster than would otherwise be possible. This is *not* the same as active transport (below) because facilitated diffusion occurs *along a concentration gradient*, and *requires no metabolic energy*.

There are two types of protein responsible for facilitated diffusion:

- Specific **carrier proteins** take particular substances from one side of the membrane to another. This is often done by **co-transport**, when an ion such as Na^+ is transported alongside the 'main' substance such as glucose.
- **Ion channels** – protein pores that can open or close to control the passage of selected ions, for example, sodium and potassium.

Osmosis

Osmosis is the diffusion of water. When two solutions are separated by a **partially permeable membrane**, which prevents at least some of the solutes moving across, water molecules will move, along *their* concentration

Examiners' Notes

Note the expression 'partially permeable' is preferred by examiners to the terms 'differentially permeable' and 'selectively permeable'.

gradient. In other words, if the solute can't diffuse to the water, the water will diffuse to the solute.

A more correct way of defining osmosis is in terms of water potential. **Water potential** is a measure of how easy it is for water to move: water in a dilute solution can move more freely than water in a concentrated solution. *Pure water* is given a water potential of 0 kPa.

Water in any solution can move less freely than in pure water, so *all* solutions have a *negative* water potential. A dilute solution will have a less negative water potential (for example, −100 kPa) than a more concentrated solution (for example, −300 kPa). If these solutions were separated by a differentially permeable membrane, water would pass from the less negative value (the dilute solution where the water can move more freely) to the more negative value (the more concentrated solution where water can move less freely). This is shown in Fig 23. The most negative water potential you are ever likely to come across is that of *dry air*. This is why water evaporates and is a vital force in the water cycle on this planet.

Examiners' Notes

Many candidates have an instinctive understanding of osmosis, but fail to gain full marks because of incorrect use of terminology. Instead of talking about 'strong' and 'weak' solutions, make sure you can describe situations in terms of water potential.

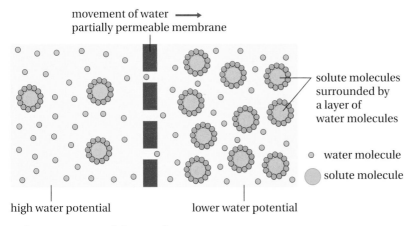

movement of water
partially permeable membrane

solute molecules surrounded by a layer of water molecules

○ water molecule

◯ solute molecule

high water potential   lower water potential

Fig 23
Osmosis occurs when two solutions of different concentration are separated by a partially permeable membrane

So the more accurate definition of osmosis is:

> **Definition**
> *Osmosis* is the movement of water from a region of less negative water potential to a region of more negative water potential across a partially permeable membrane.

Osmosis in animal cells

You should use three terms when discussing osmosis in animal cells:

- **Hypertonic** describes a solution that has a *more negative* water potential than another (it is more concentrated). For example, sea water is hypertonic to blood.

- **Isotonic** describes a solution that has the *same* water potential/concentration as another. For example, Ringer's solution can be used to keep tissues alive because it is isotonic to blood plasma.

- **Hypotonic** describes a solution that has a *less negative* water potential than another (it is less concentrated). For example, pure water is hypotonic to blood so, when we drink it, water is absorbed into our blood.

Animal cells are not surrounded by a strong cell wall. So, when they are placed in a solution of higher water potential, such as pure water, they swell up and burst. For this reason animals need to **osmoregulate** – they need to control the concentration of their body fluids. In vertebrates the main organ of osmoregulation is the kidney.

One of the most remarkable feats of the mammalian kidney is its ability to produce urine that is hypertonic to blood. So, when water is in short supply, we can still get rid of waste without losing too much precious water.

Active transport

Diffusion, facilitated diffusion and osmosis are passive; they involve the movement of substances down a diffusion gradient and therefore do not require an input of energy. Active transport is a mechanism that allows organisms to move substances across membranes *against* a diffusion gradient, for example, to allow organisms to absorb a rare trace element, or to remove virtually all of a toxic waste. Active transport makes exchange processes *more efficient*.

Essential features of active transport mechanisms are:

- Substances move *against* a concentration gradient, i.e. from low to high.

- The process requires energy in the form of ATP.

- There are specific carrier proteins in the cell membrane.

- If respiration is inhibited, for example, by a lack of oxygen, active transport slows down or stops.

Cells adapted for active transport, such as those lining the intestine (page 16) or kidney tubule, show two key adaptations:

- **Microvilli** greatly increase the membrane surface area, which means there can be more carrier proteins.

- The presence of numerous mitochondria to provide the energy required.

Absorption of carbohydrates in the gut

The digestion of carbohydrates produces large amounts of glucose, together with some fructose and galactose. All three are monosaccharides.

Initially, when there is a lot of glucose in the gut, absorption is by diffusion. As the concentration gradient decreases a special type of facilitated diffusion known as co-transport becomes the main absorption mechanism.

Co-transport involves a particular membrane protein known as SGLUT-1. This transporter protein has two binding sites, one for glucose and another for sodium ions. These two substances are carried through the membrane together. The mechanism operates only when both substances are present. Glucose is transported far more quickly by this method than when it is transported on its own.

> ## Essential Notes
>
> Galactose is absorbed in the same way as glucose, i.e. co-transport. Fructose enters the cell from the intestinal lumen via facilitated diffusion using a different transporter protein.

Bacteria, bacterial disease and the cell membrane

Bacteria are simple, single-celled organisms (Fig 24). Their cells are described as **prokaryotic**; they are small, with very few structures (organelles) inside. In contrast, virtually all other organisms – plants, animals, fungi – are eukaryotic; they have large, relatively complex cells. About 1000 bacteria could fit into an average sized animal cell.

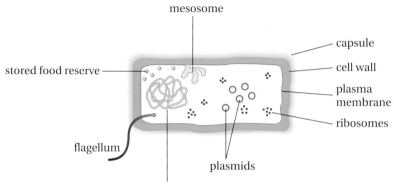

mesosome

capsule

stored food reserve

cell wall

plasma membrane

ribosomes

flagellum

plasmids

bacterial chromosome (a loop of DNA in an area called the nucleoid)

Fig 24
The basic structure of a bacterium. Notice that in prokaryotic cells there is no nuclear membrane

The life of a bacterium is pretty simple. Most absorb food by **extracellular digestion** – they make and secrete enzymes that digest any available food source, then absorb the soluble products. In doing so they increase in volume until they are ready to reproduce, which they mainly do by **binary fission**. This involves simply splitting in half. When conditions are favourable – plenty of warmth, moisture, nutrients and (usually) oxygen – they can split as frequently as every 20 minutes. Bacteria are absolutely essential in recycling and most are harmless to human health, but a few are **pathogenic**.

Cholera

Cholera is one of the most lethal of infectious diseases. Untreated, it can be fatal in just a few hours due to diarrhoea and massive fluid loss.

Cholera is caused by a bacterium, *Vibrio cholerae*. Transmission is usually via drinking water contaminated with faeces from other cholera sufferers. Cholera outbreaks occurred in the UK in Victorian times; today they are still common in the developing world. The reason is always poor sanitation and a dirty water supply.

The bacterium attaches itself to the lining of the small intestine and releases a toxin that binds to specific receptor proteins on epithelial cells of the gut wall. The toxin activates a messenger molecule, cyclic AMP, which in turn activates the CFTR protein – a chloride pump in the cell membrane.

Normally, this pump acts like a gate for water – it closes and opens to regulate the amount of water in the intestine. In the presence of the cholera toxin, the CFTR protein is fixed into an open position, causing the cells to lose chloride ions at a massive rate. Sodium ions follow (positive ions follow the negative ions). The result of this massive loss of salt is that water follows by osmosis. Large amounts of water pass out of the cells and the body, resulting in watery diarrhoea often described as 'rice water stool'.

This is much worse than ordinary diarrhoea. In most cases of 'the runs', the irritated gut wall simply pushes out faeces faster than normal, so that the water has no time to be absorbed from the gut. Cholera is much worse: the toxin effectively makes the gut wall freely permeable, so that fluid just pours out of the body through the intestine.

This can be fatal very rapidly because the body becomes dehydrated and some vital ions such as sodium, chloride and potassium become very depleted. Children and the elderly are at high risk of dying. Treatment must be given quickly – it is more important to solve the dehydration first by either drinking a lot of water, or, if the victim is really weak, by **rehydration therapy** through a drip. Antibiotic treatment is then very effective, although resistant strains of the cholera bacterium are now common. Cholera is still endemic in many countries, though the mortality rate is low if rehydration treatment is given in time.

Oral rehydration solutions (ORS)

Each day the average person consumes about 2–3 litres of fluid in one form or another, and we also secrete a large volume of fluid – up to 8 litres – into our intestines in the form of digestive juices. Diarrhoeal diseases such as dysentery and cholera do not allow the efficient reabsorption of this fluid, and so the body loses water and important ions – called electrolytes – such as sodium, potassium, chloride and calcium.

Oral rehydration solutions (ORS) simply replace the lost water and ions. They also contain sugars – usually glucose – because the body needs a source of energy and – as seen above – glucose and salt are absorbed together by co-transport. Generally, ORS have a slightly higher water potential than body fluids, which means they are hypotonic to human plasma.

Essential Notes

It's quite simple to make an effective ORS using water, glucose and salt. A basic recipe is as simple as 8 teaspoonfuls of sugar and one of salt in a litre of water.

Developing new ORS – an example of how science works

There is a vast global market for ORS, and pharmaceutical companies compete to introduce new and improved versions. New ORS need to pass through human trials before they can go to market. When trialling new treatments, certain guidelines should be followed:

- The people taking part should be **volunteers**.

- **Informed consent** should be given, which means people should be made fully aware of the risks involved before agreeing to take part.

- Researchers should take all possible precautions to minimise risks to the trial participants, and there should be no chance of permanent damage from the treatment.

- Research should be carried out only by competent, experienced professionals.

- All results should enter the public domain so that successful treatments can be made widely available.

However, there are times when some guidelines might need to be ignored in the interests of the patients. For instance, the patients may be too young to give their own consent, or in developing countries there may not be enough qualified medical staff to carry out the trials (see question 5). In an epidemic or other emergency situation experimental treatments may need to be given in order to save many lives.

3.1.4 **The lungs of a mammal also act as an interface with the environment. Lung function may be affected by pathogens and by factors relating to lifestyle.**

This section is about lungs and lung disease. First, we look at breathing in humans. The basic structure of the lungs is shown in Fig 25 and the bronchial tree is shown in Fig 26.

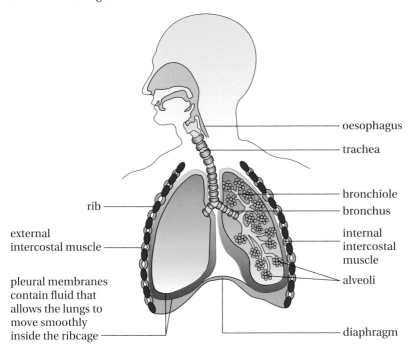

Fig 25
Basic structure of the lungs

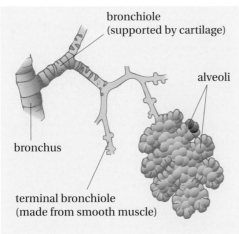

Fig 26
The bronchial tree. Note that the terminal bronchioles are made from smooth muscle and not supported by cartilage. Asthma is caused by a contraction in the smooth muscle, obstructing the passage of air in and out of the alveoli. In particular, it is difficult to breathe out. That's what causes the wheezing sound

Breathing in humans

Lungs have two basic functions:

- They get as much air as possible into close contact with blood. They do this by having millions of tiny air sacs – **alveoli** – surrounded by a dense network of blood capillaries (Fig 27).

- They **ventilate** the gas exchange surfaces – the alveoli – so they have a constant supply of fresh air with high oxygen and low carbon dioxide concentration.

Fig 27
Alveoli with capillary showing the short distance over which oxygen and carbon dioxide have to diffuse

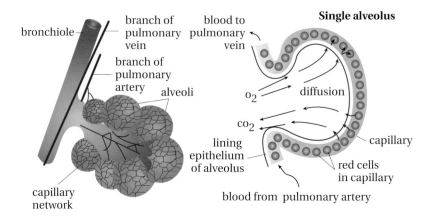

Air that enters the lungs passes down the bronchial tree through large tubes (**trachea, bronchi**) into progressively smaller ones (first **bronchioles**, then **terminal bronchioles**) and finally into the alveoli. Gas exchange takes place across the alveolar walls and the capillary walls.

Examiners' Notes

The alveolar wall is made from thin, flat cells classified as **simple squamous epithelium**. This aids rapid diffusion by presenting as thin a barrier as possible between blood and air.

Definition

Ventilation is the act of pumping fresh air in and out of the lungs, over the gas exchange surfaces, so that a diffusion gradient is maintained.

The mechanism of ventilation

Mammalian lungs contain no muscle, so cannot move on their own. Ventilation is brought about by the **intercostal** muscles and the **diaphragm**.

This is what happens when we breathe in:

- Nerve impulses pass down nerves from the **respiratory centre** in the **medulla** of the brain to the external intercostal muscles and the diaphragm.

- Contraction of the external intercostal muscles pulls the ribs up and out while the diaphragm flattens, pushing the abdominal organs downwards.

- The volume of the thorax increases, lowering the pressure below that of the atmosphere, so air is forced into the lungs.

> **Definitions**
>
> **Breathing: some key definitions**
>
> **Tidal volume** = the volume of air inhaled/exhaled in each breath. 500 cm^3 is an average value for human tidal volume while at rest.
>
> **Ventilation rate** = the number of breaths in one minute. 14 would be an average value while at rest.
>
> **Pulmonary ventilation** = Tidal volume × Ventilation rate
>
> Using the above values we get a value for pulmonary ventilation of 7000 cm^3 per minute or, more simply, 7 litres per minute.

Breathing out is largely a *passive* process – it does not require muscular contraction unless we want to speed up the process. Elastic recoil of the abdominal muscles, along with the weight of the ribcage and pressure of abdominal organs, decreases the volume of the thorax. This, together with the natural elastic recoil of the lung tissue, increases pressure inside the lungs and air is forced out through the bronchial system.

> **Examiners' Notes**
>
> Remember that when volume increases, pressure decreases and vice versa.

Lung disease

You need to know about four lung diseases: **fibrosis**, **tuberculosis**, **emphysema** and **asthma**. Examiners may use questions on these diseases as an opportunity to test your understanding of normal lung function.

Fibrosis

Fibrosis is a process by which normal tissues of an organ suffer damage and are replaced by fibrous connective tissue: 'scar tissue'. The delicate alveoli of the lungs are particularly vulnerable to fibrosis. Widespread fibrosis due to smoking or other air pollution is called emphysema, while tuberculosis can leave small patches of fibrosis caused by bacterial infection. Thus, fibrosis is a consequence of disease rather than a disease in its own right.

Tuberculosis (TB)

TB is a bacterial disease of the lungs caused by two species: *Mycobacterium tuberculosis* and *Mycobacterium bovis*. Symptoms include a persistent cough, blood-smeared sputum, shortness of breath, fever and, in the long term, weight loss.

TB is a serious global health problem. Every year 8–10 million people catch TB and 2 million die from it. About a third of the world's population, around 2 billion people, carry the TB bacteria but most never develop the active disease. TB is the commonest cause of death among AIDS patients, where it is an **opportunistic infection**, taking advantage of the individual's weakened immune system. **Drug resistant** TB is becoming more of a problem.

TB primarily affects the lungs and if the immune system does not manage to contain the infection, it can then spread, with **secondary infections** in the lymph nodes, bones and gut. TB infection is transmitted via airborne droplets, or (more rarely) via unpasteurised milk. Once TB infection is confirmed (by analysis of sputum samples), treatment usually consists of isolation of the patient during the infective stage (2–4 weeks) and the use of a combination of antibiotics for a period of six months.

In a person with a healthy immune system, the presence of the bacteria stimulates a response that attempts to stop the bacteria from spreading. Patches of infection become surrounded by white cells and then scar tissue, which isolates the bacteria, preventing them from spreading to other parts of the lung. This scar tissue is detectable by radiography and shows up as dark shadows on an x-ray.

These patches become **tubercles**, hence the name of the disease. Bacteria and white cells in the centre of these tubercles die and the infection is contained in an inactive state. Such a person typically has no symptoms and cannot spread TB to other people. Most people infected by TB have **latent** disease. The scar tissue and lymph nodes may eventually harden due to the deposition of calcium from the blood. In the long term, therefore, TB leaves the individual with patches of fibrosis and **calcified** scar tissue, which reduces the overall surface area for gas exchange.

Fig 28
Healthy alveoli above compared to an individual with emphysema below. Note the decrease in surface area and the thicker walls – classic symptoms of emphysema

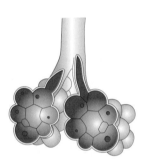

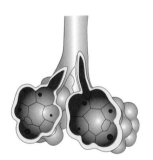

Emphysema

Emphysema is permanent lung damage (see 'fibrosis' above) caused by smoking and air pollutants. The delicate alveolar walls become damaged and replaced with connective tissue. The result is twofold:

- There is a loss of surface area and a thickening of the alveolar walls, making gas exchange less efficient.

- There is a loss of **elasticity**. Normal lungs are elastic and will exhale of their own accord, with very little muscular effort needed from the lungs or diaphragm. Emphysemic patients have to make more of an effort to breathe out.

The main cause is smoking – 80% of cases of emphysema occur in people who smoke. Emphysema usually affects older people as it is due to cumulative damage over a long period, such as a lifetime of smoking.

Asthma

Asthma is the most common lung disease, affecting an estimated 5.2 million people in the UK alone. Asthma is a difficulty in breathing caused by a constriction of the smooth muscle that makes up the terminal bronchioles (see Fig 26). The muscular walls swell and secrete more mucus than normal.

During an asthma attack the flow of air is reduced, so ventilation is less efficient. The actual surface area of the alveoli is unchanged, and people can recover from asthma with no damage to the lungs whatsoever. Asthma is not like TB and emphysema, where fibrosis occurs.

The smooth muscle usually contracts due to an allergic reaction, a reaction to exercise, air pollution and cold air. Stress can also trigger an attack. The standard asthma treatments include **antihistamines** and **steroids** to reduce the allergic response and **bronchodilators** to relax the smooth muscle in the airways.

3.1.5 The functioning of the heart plays a central role in the circulation of blood and relates to the level of activity of an individual. Heart disease may be linked to factors affecting lifestyle.

This section is about hearts and what happens when they go wrong.

Heart structure and function

Mammals have a double circulation; a **pulmonary circulation** and a **systemic circulation**.

The pulmonary circulation takes blood on the relatively short return journey to the lungs, where blood is oxygenated. When blood passes through a system of capillaries it loses pressure, so it must return to the heart for a pressure boost before it enters the systemic circulation, which takes blood around the rest of the body.

The mammalian heart acts as the pump for both the pulmonary and the systemic systems. It has four chambers; two **atria** and two **ventricles** (Fig 29). All chambers have approximately the same volume, so with each heartbeat an equal volume of blood passes to the lungs and to the whole of the rest of the body. **Atrioventricular** (AV) **valves** prevent backflow of blood from ventricles to atria. **Semilunar valves** prevent backflow of blood from arteries into ventricles.

Fig 29
(a) The structure of the heart
(b) The conducting pathway of the heart. The arrows show the direction of the impulse that causes the cardiac muscles to contract

(a)

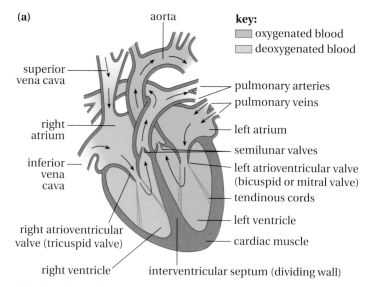

key:
☐ oxygenated blood
☐ deoxygenated blood

(b)

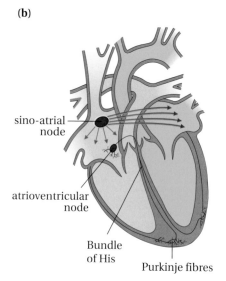

Each heartbeat is known as the **cardiac cycle**. This can be divided into three stages:

1. Both atria contract – the **atrial systole** – this takes about 0.1 seconds.

2. Both ventricles contract – the **ventricular systole** – this takes about 0.3 seconds.

3. All chambers relax – the **diastole** – this lasts about 0.4 seconds.

The regular beating of the heart is not under the control of the brain, although impulses from the brain modify the heart rate, making it faster or slower.

It is important to remember what is cause and what is effect in the heart. The electrical impulses initiate muscular contraction, the contraction squeezes the blood, increasing the pressure and forcing blood in a particular direction. This blood flow opens or closes valves. The valves are just tough flaps of tissue – they do not open and close on their own.

So, the cardiac cycle takes about 0.8 seconds in total, resulting in a heart rate of 75 beats per minute – about average for a young, resting person. The heart rate speeds up during exercise, and the safe maximum for humans is 220 beats per minute minus your age. Therefore, the maximum safe heart rate for a healthy 20-year-old would be 200.

Examiners' Notes

Make sure that you can label a section through the heart, including the chambers, valves and blood vessels.

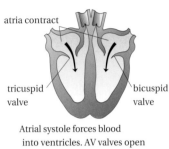

atria contract

tricuspid valve

bicuspid valve

Atrial systole forces blood into ventricles. AV valves open

ventricles contract

Atria relax, ventricles contract, AV valves close, SL valves open. Blood goes into aorta and pulmonary artery

atria and ventricles relaxed

Atria begin to refill. Ventricles are in diastole

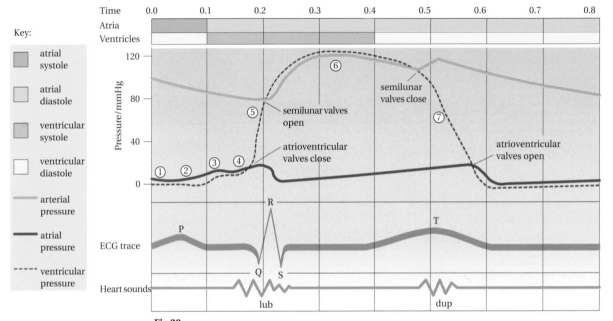

Fig 30

The events of the cardiac cycle – each numbered event is described in the text

The events of the cardiac cycle (Fig 30) can be summarised as follows:

1 Both atria fill with blood.

2 An electrical impulse, originating from the **sino-atrial node (SAN)**, spreads over the atria via specialised muscle cells, causing atrial contraction. The impulse cannot pass directly to the ventricles; there is a band of non-conducting tissue that separates the atria and the ventricles.

3 The pressure in the atria rises. Blood is forced through the atrioventricular valves, into the ventricles.

4 The impulse from the SAN stimulates the **atrioventricular node** (AVN) to produce impulses that are channelled down into the ventricles by the **bundle of His**. From here impulses pass to all parts of the ventricular wall in the **Purkinje fibres**. This pathway causes a delay that gives the ventricles time to fill with blood.

5 The ventricles contract. Blood is forced upwards, closing the AV valves and causing the first heart sound, known as 'lub'. At this point the pressure in the ventricles rises.

6   When the pressure in the ventricles exceeds that in the aorta and pulmonary artery, blood is forced through the semilunar valves.

7   As the ventricles relax, the pressure falls below that in the aorta, so the semilunar valves close again, causing the second heart sound (dup).

Meanwhile, the atria fill with blood again and the cycle repeats itself.

The control of heartbeat

The heart is **myogenic**, meaning that the muscle contraction originates from within the heart muscle itself. So, when the nerves leading to the heart are severed, it continues to beat at a slow, regular pace, but cannot be matched to the changing needs of the body. The **cardiovascular centre** in the medulla of the brain *modifies* the rate of beating (Fig 31). The cardiovascular centre receives information from two main sources:

- From **chemoreceptor** (chemical-sensitive) cells in the wall of the carotid artery and aorta – the higher the carbon dioxide concentration, the more frequently nerve impulses travel from the chemoreceptors to the medulla. Note that the body does not normally respond to a lack of oxygen – it's the build-up of carbon dioxide (and the pH change this causes) that is vital.

- From **baroreceptor** (pressure-sensitive) cells in the carotid sinus which transmit impulses to the cardiovascular centre when blood pressure rises.

Examiners' Notes

You must be able to interpret graphs such as the one in Fig 30 without the labels. You should be able to label the points at which the valves open and close. For instance, the semilunar valves open when the pressure in the ventricles exceeds the pressure in the arteries.

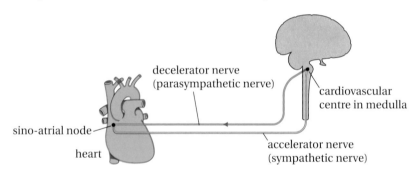

sino-atrial node

heart

decelerator nerve (parasympathetic nerve)

cardiovascular centre in medulla

accelerator nerve (sympathetic nerve)

Fig 31
Two nerves pass from the cardiovascular centre to the heart. If these nerves are cut, the heart continues to beat but the rate cannot be modified

Essential Notes

The term **antagonistic** means 'opposing effects' and can apply to nerves, muscles or hormones.

Examiners' Notes

Remember that the brain only modifies the rate of heartbeat.

Essential Notes

Carbon dioxide is an acidic gas. A build-up of carbon dioxide therefore lowers the pH of a solution

The biological basis of heart disease

Cardiovascular disease is the biggest single cause of death in the UK. It accounts for over a quarter of all deaths – about 175 000 per year. The common underlying cause of cardiovascular disease is a build-up of a fatty material, called **atheroma**, in the walls of arteries (Fig 32 overleaf).

Fig 32
The build-up of atheroma in an artery. Atheroma builds up under the endothelium (lining) of the artery, causing a narrowing and a roughening of the wall. This reduces blood flow and increases the chance of blood clots forming and lodging in the lumen

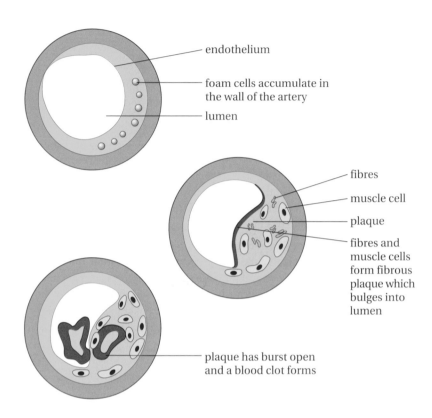

endothelium

foam cells accumulate in the wall of the artery

lumen

fibres

muscle cell

plaque

fibres and muscle cells form fibrous plaque which bulges into lumen

plaque has burst open and a blood clot forms

Definitions

Cardiovascular disease: some key definitions

Aneurysm – a ballooning of an artery due to a weakness in the wall. This requires urgent surgery because a ruptured aneurysm is usually fatal.

Angina – chest pains causes by an inadequate supply of blood (and therefore oxygen) to the heart muscle.

Arteriosclerosis – hardening of the arteries. Associated with old age, the blood vessel walls, particularly of the arteries, become less elastic and more liable to rupture.

Atheroma – the fatty deposit that builds up under the endothelium (lining) of blood vessels. As the atheroma gets thicker, the lumen of the artery gets smaller.

Atherosclerosis – a build-up of atheroma in the blood vessels.

Embolism – a clot/thrombus travelling in the bloodstream.

Myocardial infarction – scientific term for a heart attack. Part of the heart muscle – the **myocardium** – dies (infarcts) when the blood supply to that area is blocked.

Thrombosis – a blood clot (thrombus) lodged in a vessel.

Overall, atherosclerosis causes disease in two ways:

- by narrowing or even blocking vital blood vessels, such as the coronary arteries which supply blood to the heart muscle

- by initiating the formation of blood clots. An atheroma makes blood vessel walls rough and more likely to initiate clot formation. A blood clot can be fatal if it lodges in a coronary artery (leading to a heart attack) or in the brain (leading to a stroke).

Risk factors in the development of heart disease

The build-up of atheroma is usually the result of a combination of risk factors, both environmental and genetic.

Diet and blood cholesterol

Cholesterol is a perfectly natural substance, all cells contain some cholesterol and some cells have quite a lot. So it's not a deadly poison, it's important. These are the essential facts about cholesterol:

- Your body can make its own cholesterol, but it's also found in lots of the foods we eat.

- Eggs, cream and fatty meat are especially high in cholesterol. Note that these are all *animal products* – there's very little cholesterol in plants.

- High levels of cholesterol in the blood lead to a build-up of atheroma.

- Some unlucky people have a high level of cholesterol - it's genetic. These people have to watch what they eat.

- Cholesterol is a lipid, so it doesn't dissolve in water. So in order to be transported in the blood, cholesterol has to be attached to protein molecules, called **lipoproteins**. There are two types of lipoproteins, **high density (HDLs)** and **low density (LDLs)**.

- LDLs are 'bad cholesterol'. LDLs are carrying cholesterol from the liver and taking it to other cells in the body. This is when it can lead to build-up of atheroma in arteries.

- HDLs are 'good cholesterol'. They 'mop up' cholesterol and take it in the opposite direction; from body cells to the liver.

- It's all about balance. You want a high ratio of HDL to LDL.

Smoking

There is a well-established link between smoking and atherosclerosis, although the exact mechanism is complex. Certain substances in tobacco smoke constrict arteries, raising blood pressure.

High blood pressure

High blood pressure or **hypertension** can be the result of several factors: high salt intake, smoking, obesity and a genetic tendency.

Examiners' Notes

Don't call HDL and LDL good and bad cholesterol in the exam.

Examiners' Notes

Other risk factors include obesity and a lack of excercise.

3.1.6 Mammalian blood possesses a number of defensive functions.

This section is about defence against disease. The body defends itself against invading microorganisms by putting up barriers to keep them out, and then having mechanisms to deal with those that do enter.

An overview of the body's defences is shown in Fig 33 (overleaf).

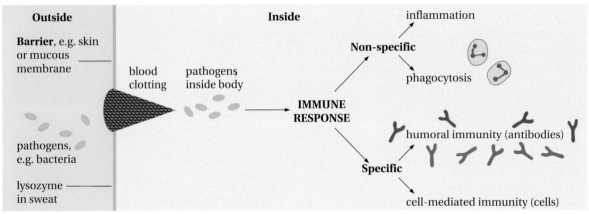

Fig 33
An overview of the body's defences: non-specific responses are general responses to damage. They include **inflammation** and **phagocytosis** of debris. Specific responses are targeted against individual types of microorganism

Phagocytosis

In this process, the most common type of white cells, the **neutrophils**, engulf any foreign material that has entered the body, such as small particles of dust in the lungs, or bacteria at the site of infection. Fig 34 shows the essential stages of phagocytosis.

Fig 34
Phagocytosis

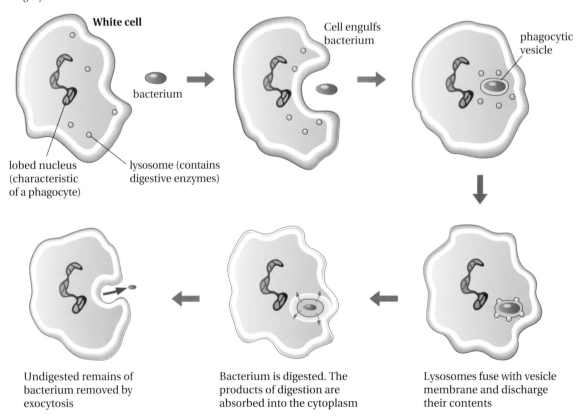

The specific immune system

This aspect of immunity involves the recognition of specific pathogens. For example, if the polio virus gets into the body, the immune system will respond by producing antibodies specific for that virus, and not other viruses.

There are two types of specific immune response: **cell-mediated** and **humoral** (or **antibody-mediated**), which are described in Fig 35.

Examiners' Notes

In examination answers about the immune system there is too much talk of 'fighting'. Try to avoid this description.

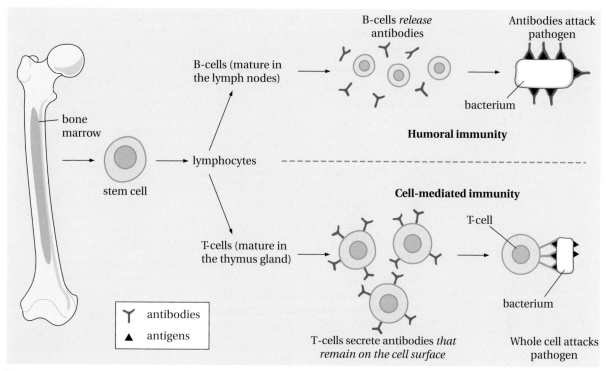

B-cells *release* antibodies

Antibodies attack pathogen

bone marrow

B-cells (mature in the lymph nodes)

bacterium

Humoral immunity

lymphocytes

stem cell

Cell-mediated immunity

T-cell

T-cells (mature in the thymus gland)

bacterium

Y antibodies
▲ antigens

T-cells secrete antibodies *that remain on the cell surface*

Whole cell attacks pathogen

Fig 35
The difference between humoral and cell-mediated immunity

Definitions

Immunity: some key definitions

An **antigen** *is a substance – usually a protein or carbohydrate – that is not normally found in the host's body. The outer surface of any pathogen is recognised as foreign because it is made up of many antigens. Antigens stimulate the production of corresponding antibodies.*

An **antibody** *is a protein made by the host's B-cells in response to a particular antigen. The antibody can combine with the antigen, and in some way neutralises the pathogen.*

Examiners' Notes

Many candidates lose marks because they cannot distinguish between antigen and antibody.

Both types of specific immune response involve the recognition of specific antigens and the production of tailor-made antibodies:

- In cell-mediated immunity the whole cell attacks the pathogen; cell mediated means 'carried out by the cells'.

- In humoral immunity the antibodies produced by the cell attack the pathogen. Humoral means 'of the fluid' and refers to the fact that the antibodies in the plasma (fluid) attack the pathogen.

The primary and secondary immune response

The immune response involves the production of particular antibodies in response to a pathogen/antigen. There are two phases: primary and secondary.

In the **primary immune response**, B lymphocytes (or B-cells) – one type of white blood cell – are made and mature in the bone marrow (hence the B). It is thought that at birth there are thousands of small populations – or clones – of B cells, each one being capable of producing a particular antibody. When a pathogen (or antigen) gets into the body for the first time, it stimulates the relevant clone to multiply rapidly into plasma cells and memory cells:

- **Plasma cells** are short-lived cells that circulate in the blood and secrete large amounts of antibodies. Plasma cells are all clones of the same cell, so all make the same antibody.

- **Memory cells** are long-lived cells that may exist for many years.

The primary immune response may not be strong enough to prevent disease symptoms completely. Once the memory cells are in place, however, any further exposure to the antigen will stimulate the **secondary immune response**, in which the memory cells rapidly multiply into a large population of plasma cells. This ensures that enough antibody can be produced to prevent infection before symptoms develop.

The difference between the primary and the secondary responses is shown in Fig 36 (overleaf). The second exposure to an antigen results in a faster, greater and more prolonged production of antibodies.

Essential Notes

White blood cells are sometimes just called white cells because many of them spend most of their time out of the blood. White cells are also generally known as leucocytes, while red blood cells are known as erythrocytes.

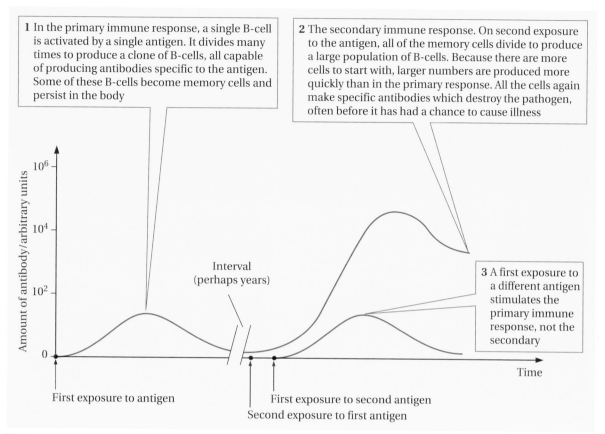

1 In the primary immune response, a single B-cell is activated by a single antigen. It divides many times to produce a clone of B-cells, all capable of producing antibodies specific to the antigen. Some of these B-cells become memory cells and persist in the body

2 The secondary immune response. On second exposure to the antigen, all of the memory cells divide to produce a large population of B-cells. Because there are more cells to start with, larger numbers are produced more quickly than in the primary response. All the cells again make specific antibodies which destroy the pathogen, often before it has had a chance to cause illness

3 A first exposure to a different antigen stimulates the primary immune response, not the secondary

Interval (perhaps years)

First exposure to antigen

First exposure to second antigen
Second exposure to first antigen

Fig 36
The primary and secondary immune responses

Passive and active immunity

- In **active immunity** individuals make their own antibodies.

- In **passive immunity** individuals get their antibodies ready made, usually from their mother.

The big problem with the immune response is that, as stated above, an individual is often not able to prevent an infection unless it has encountered the pathogen before. This would seem to leave young babies very vulnerable, and likely to die from the first infection they encounter. Help comes from the mother, who gives her baby antibodies in two ways:

- across the placenta before birth

- in her milk after birth – antibodies are proteins and you might think that they would be digested, but the baby's gut is adapted to absorb the antibodies unchanged.

Note that passive immunity can be given in another way – by an **antiserum** that contains particular antibodies. For instance, snake bites can be treated with antisera containing antibodies that neutralise the snake toxin. This is not the same as a **vaccine**, which does not contain antibodies. Antisera provide instant antibodies to cope with a crisis. In contrast, vaccines work in the long term, enabling an individual to make their own antibodies.

> **Definition**
>
> An *antiserum* is a sample of serum that contains particular antibodies.

Vaccinations

Humans have survived for thousands of years, without medical help, this being a relatively recent development. However, until the 20th century, infant mortality was very high throughout the world. A large proportion of children – up to 50% or more – did not survive until their fifth birthday because of a combination of infectious disease and malnutrition. A major step towards reducing infant mortality in developed countries was the development of vaccines.

Vaccines usually contain either the pathogen or the antigens, treated so that they cannot cause the disease. The idea is to stimulate the primary response, so that when the actual pathogen is encountered, the secondary response is strong enough to prevent the disease developing.

There are several different types of vaccine:

- **Live, attenuated vaccines** – these contain pathogens that have been treated in some way so that they can divide a few times in the body but cannot set up an infection. Measles, mumps and rubella can all be prevented by live vaccines.
- **Dead microorganisms** – these obviously cannot cause the disease but they contain the antigens that stimulate the immune response, e.g. diphtheria.
- **Purified antigens** – often made by genetic engineering (see Unit 2), for example, hepatitis B.

The problems with flu vaccines

The influenza virus shows **antigenic variation**. It is able to change the proteins on its outer coat. Each new strain of virus that emerges has different antigens, and so any antibodies made in response to previous strains are no use. This is why vulnerable people such as the elderly are offered flu vaccines every winter.

The use of monoclonal antibodies

Antibodies are very specific, and can be made to bind to almost any substance, which gives them a variety of uses, for example, in cancer treatment, or analytical tests such as pregnancy tests. **Monoclonal antibodies** (MABS) are antibodies that can be produced in large amounts in the laboratory, from a single clone of cells.

The basic process of making monoclonal antibodies involves fusing an antibody-making cell (a lymphocyte) with a certain type of tumour cell. The resulting hybrid cell will divide and divide many times, making large amounts of the required antibody.

Essential Notes

A **vaccine** is the actual fluid that is injected or swallowed. **Vaccination** is the process of administering the vaccine. The terms **vaccination** and **immunisation** basically refer to the same process.

How Science Works

In science, we make advances by a combination of two processes:

1 **Observation** We look at the world and say 'Could it possibly be...?' and then come up with testable ideas. We call these **hypotheses**.

2 **Experimentation** We gather evidence and analyse the data to draw reliable conclusions. Sometimes we gather support for our hypothesis, and sometimes we disprove it. Importantly, we never, ever, prove anything. So don't write this in your conclusions.

From your practical investigations in biology you will already be familiar with many of the basic principles used by scientists in their research. The following rules should be applied to any scientific investigation.

Testing a hypothesis

Fig H1 summarises the stages in scientific research.

Progress in science is made when a hypothesis is tested by an experiment. Contrary to popular belief, scientists do not just do experiments to see what

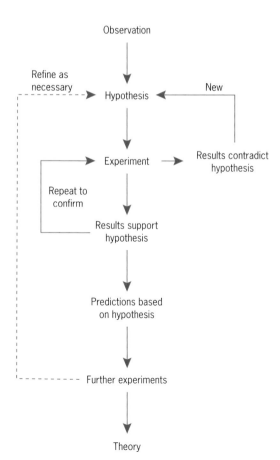

Fig H1
The stages of scientific research

happens. Fun though it might be, they don't just mix chemicals together and watch the results.

An experiment must be designed to test one possible explanation of an observation. The definition of a good hypothesis is that an experiment can either support or disprove it. Strictly, experiments can never prove that a hypothesis is absolutely, definitely correct. There is always the possibility that another explanation, one that no one has thought of, could fit the evidence equally well. However, an experiment can prove that a hypothesis is definitely wrong.

Unfortunately, people are often tempted to bypass the testing stage and go straight to an explanation without obtaining any experimental evidence. Some people seem to be uncomfortable when they are unable to find an explanation for a phenomenon. Even scientists have a tendency to be biased towards finding evidence to support their hypothesis.

As a student, you may well have done an investigation during which you were disappointed to get results that disproved your hypothesis. Or maybe your results were not what you expected. When this happens students often suggest that their experiment has 'gone wrong', but, in scientific research, negative results are just as important as positive ones.

When does a hypothesis become an accepted theory?

A hypothesis only becomes accepted theory when it has been thoroughly tested. The hypothesis may suggest predictions that, in turn, can be tested by further experiments and observations. Other scientists try to think of alternative interpretations of the results. It is normal practice for one scientist to be critical of another's published results. To ensure that published work is of sufficiently high quality, journals practise **peer review** – a submitted paper is reviewed by two or three other experts in the field to make sure the experiments have been carried out well, and that the way the results have been interpreted is reasonable.

Essential Notes

The term 'expert in the field' is used to describe a scientist with experience and a great deal of knowledge in a particular area of science. In peer review, the scientists reviewing their colleagues' (peers') research, need to work in the same area of science, to be able to give a reliable and useful opinion of its quality.

It should also be possible to repeat an experiment and get the same results. Only after many confirmatory experiments is it likely that a new idea will be accepted. For example, for many years it was thought that cell membranes had a structure rather like a sandwich with protein 'bread' and phospholipid 'filling'. After many experiments this hypothesis was shown to be false and it has been replaced by the fluid-mosaic explanation described in this unit. This idea is now so well supported that it is described as the theory of plasma membrane structure.

Once a hypothesis is supported in this way, by many experimental results and observations, it may be accepted as the best explanation of an observation.

A theory is, therefore, a well-established hypothesis that is supported by a substantial body of evidence. The Theory of Natural Selection, for example, is based on huge numbers of observations, predictions and experiments that support the underlying hypothesis.

Designing an investigation

Suppose you are asked to design an experiment to investigate the effect of temperature on the rate of reaction of an enzyme such as catalase.

Your hypothesis could be

Temperature has an effect on the rate of enzyme controlled reactions.

Variables and controls

Catalase breaks down hydrogen peroxide to water and oxygen. To investigate the effect of temperature on the reaction, you could set up water baths at a range of temperatures, mix the catalase and hydrogen peroxide and measure the amount of oxygen released at each temperature.

There are, of course, practical difficulties to be overcome, such as collecting the oxygen without letting any escape, but in principle the experiment is quite simple. The key to this and all similar experiments is that you do three things:

- Select and set up a range of different values for the factor whose effect you are testing, in this case temperature. This factor is the **independent variable**.

- Measure the change in the factor that you are testing, in this case the rate of oxygen production. This is the **dependent variable**.

- Keep all other factors, such as enzyme and hydrogen peroxide concentrations, the same. These are the **controlled variables**.

Including a control experiment

One other precaution is to carry out a **control** experiment. This is not the same as keeping other variables constant. Its purpose is to ensure that changes made to the independent variable have not in themselves changed any other factor, and that the results really are due to the factor being tested.

For example, in the enzyme investigation featured above, how do we know that it is the enzyme that is breaking down the substrate and not simply the effect of temperature, or some other chemical in the enzyme solution? To answer that question, we must do a control experiment in which the enzyme is first boiled (to denature it), or left out altogether. If no oxygen is produced, we have shown that it really was the enzyme that was catalysing the reaction, not another factor.

Another example of a control can be taken from the common practical to test how effectively different antiseptics kill bacteria. Paper discs soaked in the antiseptic might be placed on a bacterial lawn in a Petri dish as shown in Fig H2.

In this experiment four of the discs were soaked in different antiseptics. The fifth disc was the control. The control disc should not be just a plain paper disc, but a disc that has also been soaked in sterile water, or whatever solvent was used in the antiseptics. This would show that the results obtained were really

Examiners' Notes

- The independent variable is the one the experimenter changes. The dependent variable is the one the experimenter measures.

- All other possible variables are kept constant.

Fig H2
The effect of antiseptic discs on bacteria growth

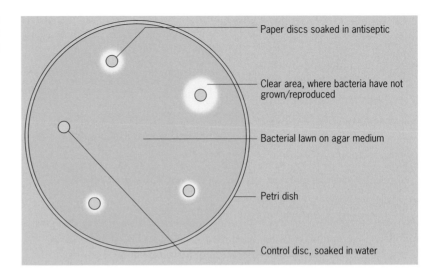

Paper discs soaked in antiseptic

Clear area, where bacteria have not grown/reproduced

Bacterial lawn on agar medium

Petri dish

Control disc, soaked in water

due to the antiseptics and not, perhaps, to something that could dissolve from the paper disc.

What happens if it is not possible to control all the variables?

Sometimes it is not easy to ensure that all the major factors have been controlled. In an experiment on enzyme activity, controlling all the variables, apart from the independent variable you want to test, is quite straightforward. However, when experimenting with living organisms, investigations are rarely so simple because living things, themselves, are so variable.

If you are measuring the response of an animal to a stimulus, such as a woodlouse to light, you can never be sure that every single woodlouse will respond in the same way. Although most woodlice will move away from light, some might not. Even the simplest of organisms respond to many stimuli. A living thing may behave untypically according to how well fed it is, its age, the time of day, its sexual maturity, or just because it is genetically different from most.

The only way to deal with this uncontrollable variability is to *repeat* an experiment several times and to use a large number of different organisms. Even in an experiment like the one using catalase it would be necessary to repeat the procedure several times for each value of the independent variable. For example, you would make several measurements of rate of oxygen production at 35 °C, several at 40 °C. Each repeat is called a **replicate**. Repetition increases the **reliability** of the results, and this increases the likelihood of being able to draw **valid** conclusions.

For students, there is nearly always a limit to the number of times an experiment can be repeated. Even researchers have time and resource constraints, and it is necessary to use judgement about the likely reliability of a set of data. If the results from replicates are all very similar, it is more likely that the results are reliable.

Accuracy and limitations

There is a limit to the accuracy of any measurement made in the course of an experiment. One limiting factor is the accuracy of the measuring instrument. A second is the care with which the instrument is used. But in biological experiments there is often a practical limit to the accuracy that it is worth trying to achieve. Although instruments exist which can measure length to a fraction of a micrometre, there would be no point in such accuracy when measuring tail length in mice in an investigation of variation. In fact, with a wriggling mouse, it might be difficult to measure even to the nearest millimetre. This difficulty would be compounded by having to decide exactly where the base of the tail actually starts. It is important, therefore, to consider the accuracy that might reasonably be expected from a set of data.

Accuracy is often confused with reliability. Consider the data in Table H1.

Leaf	Loss in mass over 24 hours/g	
	Plant A	Plant B
1	1.03	0.28
2	0.96	0.72
3	0.89	0.74
4	1.05	0.69
5	0.94	0.64
Mean	0.968	0.64

Table H1
Comparing loss in mass of leaves from two different types of plant

Taking measurements from several specimens increases the reliability of the results, but it does not make them more accurate. For plant A, all the results are reasonably similar, which suggests that the value for the mean is probably quite reliable. However, if another five leaves were measured, it is highly unlikely that exactly the same mean would be obtained.

The mean is given to 3 significant figures, but the results only to 2 significant figures. It is clearly absurd to give a value for the mean that is more precise than the accuracy of the measurements. Calculators give answers to many places of decimals, but judgement has to be used about the number of significant figures that can sensibly be given in data for means, or other calculations that are derived by manipulating raw data.

The mean for plant B looks unreliable, to say the least. The result for Leaf 1 is very different from all of the others, so the mean comes well below all the other results. It may be that this result was a mistaken reading of the balance. On the other hand the anomaly may have been because the leaf was atypical: it may have been much smaller, with fewer stomata than normal, or half-dead, for example. Without information about the original masses from which the losses were calculated it is impossible to guess. Expressing the results as percentage loss rather than as total loss would make comparison more reasonable.

Associations and correlations: What affects what?

Many biological investigations depend on a combination of observation and data analysis rather than on actual experiments. This is because it is often not practical to carry out proper controlled experiments with living organisms in the field. There are two reasons for this:

- Logistical reasons. The complexity of interrelationships between organisms and the environment makes it virtually impossible.

- Ethical reasons. It is, for example, not ethical to remove the whole population of one species in an ecosystem in order to find the effect on the food web. Similarly you can't experiment on the effects of smoking by taking two groups of people and making one group smoke and the other group not, while keeping all other factors the same.

Investigators, therefore, have to look for associations that occur in the normal course of events. However, care needs to be taken when drawing conclusions. The number of fish in a lake affected by acid rain or some other pollutant may decline, but this does not necessarily mean that the pollution has caused the decline, or even that the two are connected. Further investigations could look for data on natural populations of particular fish species in water of different acidity. It would also be possible to carry out laboratory experiments to determine fish survival rates in water of different acidity. Results might well show that the lower the pH the lower the survival rate. In this case there would be a correlation between pH and fish survival. This would still not prove that the decline in fish numbers in the lake was actually caused by the acidity.

If you counted, say, the number of nightclubs and pubs and the number of churches in several towns and cities and then plotted a graph of one against the other you would almost certainly find a correlation. But this would obviously not prove that churches cause nightclubs and pubs to be built, or the other way round. The correlation is likely to be the result of a completely separate factor, probably the size of the town or city.

Similarly the decline in fish numbers might be due to some other factor, which might or might not be due to acidity. There could be an indirect association, caused by the effect of acidity on the food supply or the acid-related release of toxic mineral ions. A laboratory experiment would be unable to mimic the complex interaction of abiotic and biotic factors in the real situation of the lake.

Nevertheless, it is only by searching for correlations and investigating them further that biologists can increase their understanding of ecology.

In the next chapter we consider in more detail how correlations in data can be analysed.

Essential Notes

A correlation may be either positive or negative. When one factor increases as another increases it is a positive correlation; when one increases while another decreases it is a negative correlation.

Experiments on humans

This phrase may bring to mind a Frankenstein-like image but, in fact, very many experiments are done with human subjects in biology, to investigate the causes of particular diseases, and to test out potential drugs and treatments.

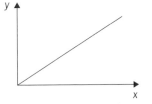

(a) Positive correlation: as x increases, y increases

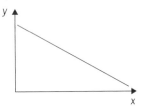

(b) Negative correlation: as x increases, y decreases

(c) As x increases, y increases up to a point, after which increasing x has no effect

Fig H3
A line graph is a simple way of showing a correlation between two variables. You should be able to look at a graph and describe it in one or two sentences.

Studying human epidemiology

It is just as hard, if not harder, to use experiments to establish links between human diseases and factors such as environmental pollutants, diet, smoking and other aspects of lifestyle as it is to test a woodlouse's response to light for example.

Most associations have been established by studying the incidence of disease or disorders in large groups of people. Looking for patterns in the occurrence of disease in human populations is called **epidemiology**. Many of the suggested links have been controversial and some have caused considerable confusion in the minds of the public. There are still some people who refuse to accept the association between smoking and lung cancer, despite the overwhelming statistical evidence. The stages in establishing the cause of a non-infectious disease are:

• Look for a correlation between a disease and a specific factor.

• Develop hypotheses that could explain how the factor might have its effect.

• Test these hypotheses to find out whether the factor can cause the disease.

Establishing a correlation involves collecting data from very large numbers of people. Because people and their lifestyles are hugely variable, it is important to make comparisons between matched groups as far as possible. For example, suppose you were looking for a correlation between beer drinking and heart disease. It would not be enough just to compare the rates of heart disease between 1000 beer drinkers and 1000 non-drinkers. The ideal comparison would be between groups of people where the only difference in lifestyle was whether or not they drank beer.

In practice this would be virtually impossible to achieve. But, if groups were matched for age, sex, amount of exercise taken and major features of diet, the comparison would be much more valid.

It is very difficult to eliminate the possibility that any correlation is not due to some other linked factor. It may be, for example, that people who like drinking beer also like eating fish and chips, and eat them often. Or, they might have a genetic predisposition to heart disease. The latter is particularly difficult to argue against: those that challenge the evidence linking smoking to lung cancer often use it to put doubt in people's minds.

Once a correlation has been found, the next stage is try to determine how the factor actually causes its effect. This is often much more difficult. Many diseases, such as heart disease and cancers develop as a result of several factors that all interact. The correlation between smoking and incidence of lung cancer has been established for many years but no single specific carcinogen in cigarette smoke has yet been identified. The tar inhaled in cigarette smoke contains a massive cocktail of hundreds of organic compounds. Many of these may have carcinogenic properties, and may affect different people in different ways. Individuals differ in their susceptibility, probably due to genetic factors.

Research on the chemicals in tar, experiments on animals and with tissue cultures, and comparisons between many genetically distinct groupings of people have been done, but the only way to avoid the carcinogenic effects of smoking is never to smoke. One day, if a precise mechanism is discovered, it may be possible to produce non-harmful cigarettes, but this seems remote.

Human clinical trials to test new drugs

Drug testing is an area where good scientific practice is vital. When testing new drugs on human patients, it is not good enough to give some patients the new drug and give nothing to the control group. The patients in the control group should get a pill that is exactly the same as the one with the new drug except for the absence of the active ingredient. A pill without any active ingredient is called a **placebo**.

Clinical trials usually involve **double-blind** investigations. The aim of these is to eliminate subjective bias on the part of both experimental subjects and the experimenters. In a double-blind experiment, neither the individuals nor the researchers know who belongs to the control group and the experimental group. Only after all the data has been obtained do the researchers learn which individuals are which. Performing an investigation in this way lessens the influence of psychological effects, such as prejudices and unintentional physical cues, on the results. Assignment of the subject to the experimental or control group must be done in a random way. The information that identifies the subjects and which group they belonged to is kept by a third party and not given to the researchers until the study is over. Double-blind methods should be applied to any trial where there is the possibility that the results will be affected by conscious or unconscious bias on the part of the experimenter.

Normally, drug trials take place in three phases:

- **A Phase I trial** is an early stage clinical trial in which an experimental drug is tested in a small number of healthy human volunteers to check if it is safe, i.e. there are no side-effects. This type of trial does not test whether a drug works against a particular disease.

- **A Phase II trial** is the next stage clinical trial in which an experimental drug that has successfully passed through a Phase I trial is tested to see if it can treat a specific disease or condition. Human volunteers with the disease or condition are given either the experimental drug or a standard drug, as a control. The groups are then compared to see which drug is the most beneficial.

- **A Phase III trial** has a similar format to a Phase II trial but involves a larger number of human patients – usually hundreds or thousands. A drug must pass successfully through Phase III trials before it can be approved for general use.

Practice exam-style questions

1   The bar graph shows some the main causes of death among UK males in 2001 and 2006.

Fig E1

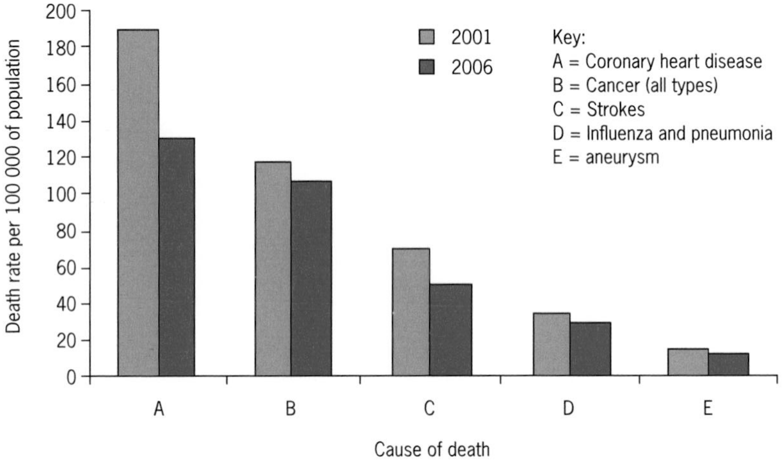

(a) Which category of disease, A–E, can be classed as a communicable disease?   1 mark

_____

(b) The population of the UK is 55 million. Calculate how many men died from coronary heart disease in 2006.
     Show your working.   2 marks

_____

_____

(c) List three risk factors associated with the development of coronary heart disease.   2 marks

_____

_____

_____

(d) Suggest two reasons for the reduction in the number of deaths, per 100 000 of population from heart disease
     from 2001 to 2006.   2 marks

_____

_____

_____

Total 7

2 The diagram shows the primary sequence of the protein lysozyme – an enzyme found in tears and sweat.

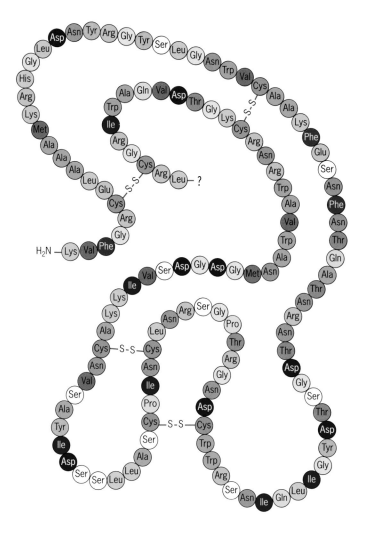

Fig E2

(a) The polypeptide chain of lysozyme has an $-NH_2$ group on one end – what chemical grouping should be at the other end? **1 mark**

Trypsin is a protein-digesting enzyme that hydrolyses proteins by making a cut in the polypeptide chain wherever an argenine (Arg) is found next to a lysine (Lys).

(b) Into how many fragments would trypsin digest lysozyme? **1 mark**

Enzymes are described as being specific.

(c) (i) What is meant by specificity?   1 mark

_____

_____

(ii) If enzymes are specific, explain how trypsin is able to digest a wide variety of different proteins, for example in pork, beef, chicken, milk and soya.   2 marks

_____

_____

_____

Total 5

3   A student carried out an investigation into the effect of pH on the activity of amylase, a starch-digesting enzyme.

The student set up seven test tubes containing starch solution and then added buffer solutions set at pH 3, 5, 7, 9 and 11. After they were thoroughly mixed, the amylase was added. At regular intervals, the student removed a drop of solution from each tube and tested for the presence of starch.

In the investigation:

(a) What was the independent variable?   1 mark

_____

(b) What was the dependent variable?   1 mark

_____

(c) State three variables that would need to be controlled.   3 marks

_____

_____

_____

(d) Describe how the student could test for the presence of starch.   2 marks

_____

_____

(e) The teacher suggested that the buffer solutions could be digesting the starch. What control experiments should be carried out to validate the results of this experiment?   2 marks

_____

_____

Total 9

4   Complete the table with ticks if the statement is true, crosses if not.

	Diffusion	Osmosis	Facilitated diffusion	Active transport
Takes place against a diffusion gradient				
Requires metabolic energy from the cell				
Requires a partially permeable membrane				
Requires specific proteins in the membrane				

Total 4

5   The following is adapted from a report on the Johns Hopkins University website.

Since its development in the 1960s, oral rehydration solution has been credited with saving the lives of millions of children throughout the world who suffer from dehydration caused by severe diarrhoea. The solution is a mixture of water, glucose, sodium, chloride and potassium, which help children recover and
5   retain vital fluids and nutrients.

A recent study showed that children given a less concentrated oral rehydration solution (one with reduced osmolarity) for the treatment of dehydration and diarrhoea are significantly less likely to need costly intravenous (IV) fluid treatment compared to children treated with the current solution used by the
10 World Health Organization (WHO).

The new reduced osmolarity solution is a less concentrated formula and contains less sodium than the current WHO solution. The lower osmolarity helps the body absorb water more quickly and reduces the risk of hypernatraemia, which is a rare but deadly disorder caused by too much salt in
15 the body.

For the double-blind study, researchers randomly selected 675 children suffering from diarrhoea from health centres in five developing countries. All of the children selected for the study were aged between one month and 24 months. Half of the group was treated with the current rehydration solution while the other half was
20 treated with the new reduced osmolarity solution.

The authors concluded that children who received the reduced osmolarity solution were 33 per cent less likely to need IV treatment when compared to the children treated with the current WHO formula. Also, the new formula was
24 equally effective at reducing diarrhoea and vomiting.

(a) Explain the term *reduced osmolarity* (line 7) in terms of water potential.   1 mark

_____

_____

(b) Suggest how the lower levels of sodium allow the body to absorb water faster. 2 marks

_____

_____

(c) Explain what is meant by a *double-blind* study (line 16). 3 marks

_____

_____

_____

(d) Explain **one** ethical issue involved in using children in clinical trials. 1 mark

_____

_____

Total 7

6 The diagram shows the heart during a particular stage of the cardiac cycle.

Fig E3

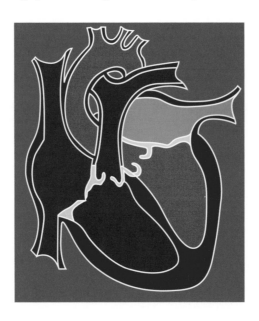

(a) Label:

(i) the atrioventricular valves

(ii) the aorta 2 marks

(b) Does this diagram show atrial systole or ventricular systole? Give one piece of evidence that supports your answer. 1 mark

_____

(c) Explain how a blood clot in a coronary artery may lead to a myocardial infarction. 2 marks

_____

_____

_____

Total 5

7 The immune system is the body system that provides defence against disease.

(a) What is meant by the term antigen? 1 mark

_____

_____

(b) Explain how a vaccine gives an individual long-term resistance against a particular disease. 4 marks

_____

_____

_____

_____

_____

(c) Explain why it is particularly difficult to develop an effective vaccine against influenza. 2 marks

_____

_____

_____

(d) Suggest why some people may object to their child being given a particular vaccination. 1 mark

_____

_____

(e) In some circumstances, people with an infection may be treated by injecting antibodies directly into the bloodstream. Explain why this might be necessary. 2 marks

_____

_____

_____

Total 10

Answers, explanations, hints and tips

Question	Answer	Marks
1 (a)	Influenza/pneumonia. (Flu is caused by a virus)	1
1 (b)	(130 deaths per hundred thousand $\times$ 10 $\times$ 55) = 71 500	2
1 (c)	Any three from; high blood pressure, obesity, smoking, high cholesterol, genetic predisposition.	2, one for two factors, two for three factors
1 (d)	Any two from; better education about risk avoidance, fewer smokers, more people exercising, earlier diagnosis and treatment.	2, one for each
		Total 7
2 (a)	–COOH	1
2 (b)	2	1
2 (c) (i)	It only catalyses one particular reaction.	1
(ii)	The proteins are different but they are still made up of the same 20 amino acids. It is possible for any of them to have an Arg next to a Lys, and so be cut by trypsin.	2
		Total 5
3 (a)	pH (the independent variable is the factor that is varied).	1
3 (b)	The rate of reaction (the time taken to digest the starch).	1
3 (c)	Any three from: Same temperature throughout; Same volume and concentration of buffer; Same volume and concentration of enzyme; Same volume and concentration of starch.	3, one for each
3 (d)	Add some (yellow/brown) iodine solution. If it goes blue/black, there is still some starch there.	2
3 (e)	Repeat the experiment with boiled enzyme. This shows that it was the enzyme, and not the buffer or any other factor, that was digesting the starch.	2
		Total 9

4

	Diffusion	Osmosis	Facilitated diffusion	Active transport
Takes place against a diffusion gradient	×	×	×	√
Requires metabolic energy from the cell	×	×	×	√
Requires a partially permeable membrane	×	√	√	√
Requires specific proteins in the membrane	×	×	√	√

1 mark for each correct column

Total 4

Question	Answer	Marks
5 (a)	Reduced osmolarity = higher water potential.	1
5 (b)	Greater water potential difference between solution and body fluids, so increased rate of osmosis.	2
5 (c)	A test where neither the patients, nor the doctors/people administering the drug, know which is the new treatment and which is the control. This eliminates differential treatment of either group.	3
5 (d)	Children are too young to give informed consent.	1
		Total 7
6 (a) (i)	Correct label, one mark each	1
6 (a) (ii)		1
6 (b)	Ventricular systole. The atrioventricular valves are closed; The semilunar valves are open.	1
6 (c)	Any two from: Part of heart muscle starved of oxygen. Heart muscle dies (infarcts). Normal contraction not possible/conducting pathway blocked.	2
		Total 5
7 (a)	A substance/protein that stimulates the production of a particular antibody; Or: A substance not normally found in the host body, that stimulates the immune response.	1
7 (b)	Any four from: Vaccine contains antigen/pathogen; Stimulates the primary immune response; Leads to the production of memory cells; If pathogen encountered, body produces antibodies quickly; Immunity lasts as long as the memory cells do;	4
7 (c)	Any two from: Virus constantly mutates/makes new strains; New proteins/antigens on surface/antigenic variation; Existing antibodies/memory cells ineffective.	2
7 (d)	Some parents perceive risk of potential side-effects, for example, allergic reaction, autism.	1
7 (e)	Any two from: When treatment is urgent/no time for body to make own antibodies; Antibody production takes time/weeks, for example, snake bites.	2
		Total 10

Glossary

Accuracy	**HSW** A measure of how close the data is to the actual true value. Note the difference between accuracy and precision. If a man is 1.81 m tall, a measurement of 1.743 m is precise but not accurate. The difference between accurate and precise is illustrated below:

 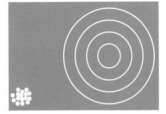  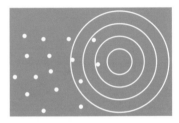

Precise-Accurate	Precise-Inaccurate	Imprecise-Accurate	Imprecise-Inaccurate

Actin	Fibrous protein found in muscles. Combines with myosin to bring about muscle contraction.
Activation energy	Energy required to start a reaction: the energy needed to break bonds in the reactants before new ones can form to make the products.
Active immunity	Immune response in which an individual makes their own antibodies to combat a particular infection. Compare with **passive immunity**.
Active site	Catalytic centre of an enzyme: pocket/groove on the surface of an enzyme into which a substrate fits. The active site and substrate have complementary shapes.
Active transport	Movement of particles across a membrane against a diffusion gradient. Requires specific membrane proteins and energy (from ATP).
Amino acid	Building block of a protein. There are 20 different amino acids in living things. All have three-letter abbreviations, for example, valine, proline, serine (Val, Pro, Ser).
Amylase	Enzyme that breaks down (hydrolyses) starch to maltose.
Amylopectin	Branched polymer of glucose: one of the two types of polysaccharide that make up starch. See also **amylose**.
Amylose	Unbranched polymer of glucose: one of the two types of polysaccharide that make up starch. See also **amylopectin**.
Aneurysm	Ballooning of an artery due to a weakness in the vessel wall. This requires urgent surgery because a ruptured (burst) aneurysm is usually fatal.
Angina	Chest pain caused by an inadequate supply of blood (and therefore oxygen) to the heart muscle.
Antagonistic	Having an opposing effect. Can apply to muscles, nerves or hormones.
Antibody	In immunity, a specific protein made by a B lymphocyte in response to a particular antigen.
Antibody-mediated immunity	Immunity 'done by antibodies' – antibodies released by B cells punch holes in target cells and pathogens, killing them. Compare with **cell-mediated immunity**.

Antigen	In immunity, a substance (usually protein) not usually found in a host's body, that stimulates the production of a specific antibody. Antigens label pathogens, or transplanted tissue, as foreign, allowing the body to tell self from non-self.
Antiserum	Preparation containing antibodies that gives an individual instant passive immunity. Useful when there is no time to develop active immunity, for example, after a snake bite.
Arteriosclerosis	Hardening of the arteries: the blood vessel walls, particularly of the arteries, become less elastic and more liable to rupture. Associated with old age.
Assimilation	Process in which an organism uses the molecules it has obtained by feeding or photosynthesis to make new body tissue.
Asthma	Lung disease in which terminal bronchioles constrict, narrowing the airways.
Atheroma	Fatty deposit that builds up under the endothelium (lining) of blood vessels. As the atheroma gets thicker, the lumen of the artery gets smaller, and the walls roughen.
Atherosclerosis	Build-up of atheroma in the blood vessels.
Atrioventricular node (AVN)	Part of the conducting pathway of the heart. The AVN picks up the signal from the sino-atrial node SAN, and delays it (allowing ventricles to fill) before passing it down into the bundle of His.
Baroreceptor	Receptor cell sensitive to changes in blood pressure. Located in the carotid sinus in the neck.
Binary fission	Simple asexual reproduction that occurs in bacteria and other single-celled organisms. One individual simply splits into two by mitosis.
Blind trial	**HSW** A trial in which the patient does not know whether they have been given the active drug or the inactive control (placebo). See also **double-blind trial**.
Brush border	Surface adapted to exchange of materials: formed from cells that possess microvilli. For example, the lining of the ileum.
Buffer solution (or Buffer)	Solution that resists any change in pH. Acids or bases can be added to a buffer and the pH will stay constant (within the limits of the buffer).
Bundle of His	Part of the conducting pathway of the heart: a bundle of specialised heart muscle fibres (*not* nerves) that transmit the impulse from the AVN to the Purkinje fibres.
Cardiovascular centre	Region in the medulla oblongata in the brain that controls heart rate.
Catalyst	Substance that speeds up a particular reaction but remains unchanged at the end of the reaction. Enzymes are biological catalysts.
Cell fractionation	Method of separating out the components of a cell to get a pure sample of nuclei, or mitochondria, for example. Usually achieved by homogenising (mashing up) cells and then using a high speed centrifuge.
Cell-mediated immunity	Immunity 'done by the cells' in which the whole cell attacks the pathogen. Compare with **antibody-mediated immunity**.
Centrifuge	Device that separates out the components of a mixture according to their density. The mixture is spun, creating a super-gravitational field. The densest component is forced to the bottom of the tube, forming the sediment. See also supernatant.

Chemoreceptor	Receptor cell sensitive to chemical change. For example, the carotid body in the neck contains chemoreceptors sensitive to carbon dioxide levels in blood plasma.
Cholesterol	Lipid component of some cell membranes. Important in the development of atheroma.
Collagen	Tough fibrous protein. Gives strength to tissues such as bone, cartilage, tendon.
Colorimeter	Device that measures intensity of colour or cloudiness (turbidity) in a solution. Gives a reading as percentage transmission or absorbance. A reference standard of pure water would give 100% transmission, or 0% absorbance.
Communicable disease	Disease that is caused by a pathogen and can be transmitted from one individual to another. Also known as infectious disease.
Condensation	Reaction in which two molecules join, forming water in the process. Carbohydrates, lipids and proteins are all made by condensation reactions.
Control	**HSW** A supplementary experiment performed as a comparison. An important way of validating an experiment.
Controlled variables	**HSW** The variables that are kept constant during an experiment, e.g. temperature, volume and concentration of reagents.
Co-transport	Transport across a cell membrane in which the movement of one substance relies on the movement of another in the same direction. For example, glucose is co-transported with sodium.
Dependent variable	**HSW** The variable that is measured as it changes during an experiment.
Diastole	Phase of the cardiac cycle in which the heart muscle is relaxed.
Dipeptide	Molecule formed when two amino acids join by a peptide link.
Disaccharide	Molecule formed when two monosaccharides join by a glycosidic link. Common examples include maltose, lactose and sucrose.
Disulphide bridge	Strong S=S bond formed in proteins: occurs where two cysteine residues are close together. Important in maintaining tertiary structure, especially in fibrous proteins, e.g. keratin.
Double-blind trials	**HSW** Trials in which neither the patients nor the researchers know who is getting the active drug and who is getting the control (placebo). Done to eliminate bias.
Embolism	Clot/thrombus travelling in the bloodstream.
Emphysema	Lung disease in which damaged alveolar walls are replaced by scar tissue.
Endocytosis	Uptake of material by a cell. Either solids (phagocytosis) or liquids (pinocytosis) are absorbed in a sphere of membrane. Opposite of exocytosis.
Enzyme–substrate complex	Combination of enzyme and substrate that exists for a very brief moment, after which there is an enzyme–product complex, and then separate enzyme and product.
Ester bond	Link between glycerol and a fatty acid found in triglycerides and phospholipids.
Eukaryotic	One of the two major cell types. Compare with prokaryotic. Eukaryotic cells are large and show more complex internal organisation and organelles.

Exocytosis	Movement of small volumes of material out of a cell. Vesicles fuse with the membrane releasing the vesicle contents outside the cell.
Exotoxin	Waste product made by a pathogen such as a bacterium. Often responsible for the symptoms of disease.
Extracellular digestion	Digestion outside the cell. Type of feeding seen in fungi and most bacteria, which make and secrete enzymes that digest the surrounding material. The soluble products are then absorbed.
Facilitated diffusion	Diffusion speeded up by specific membrane proteins. Occurs down a diffusion gradient and therefore does not need energy from the cell.
Fatty acid	An organic acid with a –COOH group. Also called a carboxylic acid. Fatty acids vary in the number of carbons in their chain and the degree of saturation (the number of C=C bonds).
Fibrosis	Response to tissue damage in which normal cells are replaced with scar tissue. See **tuberculosis**, **emphysema**.
Fluid mosaic	Model of cell membrane structure: a continuous fluid double layer of phospholipids into which a random mosaic of proteins is studded.
Glycosidic bond	Bond between two monosaccharides, for example, glucose–glucose.
High density lipoprotein: HDL	Cholesterol attached to a protein, so it can be transported in the blood. HDLs transport cholesterol from other body tissues to the liver. This is associated with a lowering of blood cholesterol levels. See also **LDL**.
Histones	In eukaryotic cells, histones are proteins that organise the DNA.
Humoral immunity	Also known as antibody-mediated immunity. When the immune response is due to the antibodies in the plasma rather then the cells themselves, as in cell-mediated immunity. (NB Humor = fluid, as in plasma).
Hydrogen bond	Weak bond formed between hydrogen atoms and electronegative atoms, usually oxygen and nitrogen. Very common and very important: H bonds are responsible for many of the properties of water and are essential in maintaining the structure of proteins and DNA.
Hydrolase	General term for any enzyme that brings about a hydrolysis reaction. Most digestive enzymes are hydrolases.
Hydrolysis	Literally, 'splitting using water'. Digestion usually involves hydrolysis.
Hydrophilic	'Water loving.' For example, the polar heads of a phospholipid, which point outwards towards water in cell membranes.
Hydrophobic	'Water hating.' For example, the non-polar tails of phospholipids, which point inwards away from water in cell membranes.
Hypertension	Medical term for high blood pressure.
Hypertonic	Having a lower water potential than another solution/cell.
Hypothesis	**HSW** An idea that it is possible to test by experiment.
Hypotonic	Having a higher water potential than another solution/cell.
Independent variable	**HSW** The variable that is tested during an experiment. For example, in 'The effect of temperature on enzyme activity', temperature is the independent variable.

Induced fit hypothesis	Model of enzyme action in which the enzyme changes its structure slightly when it combines with the substrate. Compare with the **lock and key hypothesis**.
Infectious disease	See **communicable disease**.
Inflammation	Immune response to tissue damage. The area becomes red, swollen and painful.
Interface	Point of connection. Skin, lungs and gut are all interfaces with the environment, and therefore possible routes of infection.
Isotonic	Having the same water potential as another solution/cell.
Keratin	Tough, fibrous protein found in skin, hair, nails, hooves and so on.
Lock and key hypothesis	Model of enzyme action in which the substrate fits exactly into the active site on the surface of the enzyme. Compare with **induced fit hypothesis**.
Low density lipoprotein (LDL)	Cholesterol attached to a protein, so it can be transported in the blood. LDLs transport cholesterol from the liver to other body tissues. This is associated with a raising of blood cholesterol levels. See **HDL**.
Memory cell	In immunity, a long-lived white cell (B lymphocyte) that can divide when stimulated by an antigen to bring about a secondary immune response.
Metabolism	General term for the reactions that occur inside organisms.
Micrometre (μm, or micron)	Unit of length. 10^{-6} m. 1 mm = 1000 micrometres.
Microvilli	Finger-like foldings of the cell surface membrane. Greatly increases the surface area for the exchange of materials. See also **brush border**.
Monoclonal antibody	Antibody made on a large scale for medical use, for example, in pregnancy testing or cancer therapy. Produced by a hybridoma, a B cell fused with a tumour cell. Hybridomas are immortal, divide constantly and produce large amounts of antibody.
Monomer	Individual unit in a polymer.
Monosaccharide	Single sugar. Common examples include glucose, fructose and galactose.
Myocardial infarction	Heart attack. Part of the heart muscle – the myocardium – dies (infarcts) when the blood supply to that area is blocked.
Myocardium	Heart muscle.
Myogenic	Literally, 'muscle originating'. Refers to the fact that the heartbeat is generated by the muscle itself, rather than stimulated by nerves.
Myosin	Protein found in muscle. Interacts with actin to bring about muscle contraction.
Nanometre (nm)	Unit of length. 10^{-9} m. One micrometre = 1000 nm.
Neutrophil	Most common type of white blood cell. General 'clearing up' cell whose main function is phagocytosis.
Oral rehydration solutions (ORS)	A solution of sugar and salt that combats dehydration due to diarrhoea.
Organelle	Structure within a cell, for example, mitochondrion, chloroplast, ribosome.

Organic acids	Also called carboxylic acids. They always contain the functional group –COOH. Fatty acid is the name usually given to organic acids with carbon chains longer than about eight carbons.
Osmoregulation	The control of the water potential of body fluids.
Passive	Requiring no energy input from the cell (no ATP). Contrast with active (as in **active transport**).
Passive immunity	Situation where an individual has been given antibodies (for example, from its mother, or as a treatment for snake bite) rather than made it own. See also **active immunity**.
Pathogen	A disease-causing organism. Examples include bacteria, viruses, fungi, parasites.
Peptide bond	Bond that joins two amino acids in a dipeptide.
Phagocytosis	Literally 'cell eating'. A process in which a white cell engulfs a bacterium/foreign particle and digests it, rendering it harmless.
Phospholipid	Lipid molecule consisting of one glycerol, one phosphate and two fatty acids. Key component of cell membranes.
Placebo	**HSW** A sham or fake drug given to people in the control group of a clinical trial.
Plasma cell	B lymphocyte that circulates in the blood making antibodies.
Polymer	Large molecule made from repeated units, called monomers. For example, starch is a polymer which contains glucose monomers.
Polypeptide	Chain of amino acids. Proteins are made from one or more polypeptide chains.
Polysaccharide	Large carbohydrate molecule made from repeated monosaccharide units. Starch, glycogen and cellulose are all polymers of glucose.
Polyunsaturated fatty acid	Fatty acid containing two or more C=C (double carbon) bonds.
Precision	**HSW** The closeness of repeated measurements to one another. Achieving precision involves choosing the right apparatus and using it properly. Precise readings are not necessarily **accurate** (close to the true value). A faulty piece of equipment or incorrectly used apparatus may give very precise readings (all repeated values are close together) but inaccurate (not true) results. For example, in an experiment with a colorimeter, using a dirty or scratched cuvette (sample tube) might give precise readings, but they will be highly inaccurate.
Primary immune response	Weak immune response following first exposure to an antigen/pathogen. Often not enough antibodies are produced to prevent disease symptoms. See also **secondary immune response**.
Primary structure	In a protein, the sequence of amino acids. For example, val-his-leu-his-met.
Prokaryotic	One of the two major cell types. See also eukaryotic. Prokaryotic cells are small and show much less internal organisation, no mitochondria, no ER.
Protein	Large molecules made from one or more polypeptides (polymers of amino acids). Of fundamental importance in living things.

Pulmonary circulation	The circulation that takes blood to the lungs and back. Compare with **systemic circulation**.
Purkinje fibres	Specialised cardiac muscle fibres that initiate contraction of the ventricles. This contraction begins at the apex so that blood is forced up into the arteries.
Purkyne fibres	Alternative spelling of Purkinje.
Quatenary structure	In a protein with more than one polypeptide, the overall shape of the molecule.
Random errors	**HSW** Inaccurate values lying equally above or below a true value. Can occur for many reasons, including not following a standard procedure, for example, when measuring out volumes; or using a different batch of enzyme or yeast for repeats.
Reliability	**HSW** If a measurement or test is reliable, it gives consistent results each time the activity is repeated. When undertaking an investigation a large number of repeats should ideally be taken, and any readings that vary considerably from the others (anomalous results) should be repeated.
Replicate	**HSW** A repeat: for example, an experiment that is repeated is a replicate experiment.
Respiratory centre	Region in the medulla of the brain responsible for depth and frequency of breathing.
Saturated fatty acid	Fatty acid with no C=C bonds, and therefore saturated with hydrogen.
Secondary immune response	Rapid, effective immune response to a pathogen that the body has encountered before. Memory cells, long-lived B cells, divide very rapidly in the presence of such an antigen, producing large numbers of B cells that can produce antibody specific to the infection.
Secondary structure	In a protein, the particular shape formed when the amino acid chain folds and bends. Two common examples are the ☐ helix and ☐ pleated sheet.
Sino-atrial node (SAN)	Pacemaker of the heart: a bundle of heart muscle fibres found on the wall of the right atrium that initiates the heartbeat. Modified by two nerves from the brain.
Sediment	In centrifugation, the denser material that collects at the bottom of the tube.
Substrate	Substance acted on by an enzyme, for example, the substrate for maltase is maltose.
Supernatant	In centrifugation, the fluid that remains above the sediment.
Systemic circulation	Circulation of blood around the rest of the body but not between the heart and the lungs. See also **pulmonary circulation.**
Systole	Phase of the cardiac cycle in which the heart muscle is contracted. Compare with **diastole**.
Tertiary structure	In a protein, the precise, overall, 3D shape of a polypeptide chain. Maintained by hydrogen bonds and sometimes disulphide bridges.
Thermophilic	Heat loving. Applies to bacteria that live in hot springs.
Thermostable	Resistant to break down by heat. Usually applied to a protein/enzyme that is not denatured by high temperature.
Thrombosis	Blood clot (thrombus) lodged in a vessel.

Tidal volume	Volume of air breathed in/out at rest. Average value in an adult is 500 cm^3.
Triglyceride	Lipid consisting of one glycerol molecule combined with three fatty acids.
Tubercles	Patches of fibrous tissue that develop as a result of tuberculosis. Consist of a dense mass of connective tissue that surrounds the remains of dead white cells and bacteria.
Tuberculosis	Bacterial lung disease. Causes patches of fibrosis (tubercles) in the lungs.
Turnover number	Measure of the speed of enzyme action. Defined as the number of substrate molecules turned into product by one molecule of enzyme per unit time (usually one second).
Ultracentrifugation	Centrifugation at very high speed.
Ultrastructure	Detailed structure of a cell.
Unsaturated fatty acid	Fatty acid with one C=C double bond. Can accept more hydrogen, so is unsaturated by hydrogen. See also **saturated** and **polyunsaturated fatty acids**.
Vaccine	Preparation made to stimulate a primary immune response. Contains antigens or pathogens, treated so that they don't cause the disease. Once vaccinated, exposure to the pathogen brings about the secondary immune response.
Validity	**HSW** The confidence that researchers put in a set of results and the conclusions drawn from those results. Results are valid if they measure what they are supposed to, and if they are **precise, accurate** and **reliable** (repeatable). Valid results are obtained through precise, repeatable measurements or observations, made with apparatus and experimental procedures that are suitable for the task.
Ventilation rate	Volume of air breathed in/out in one minute. At rest tidal volume × number of breaths.
Vesicle	Small sphere of membrane inside a cell. Usually used to transport substances, for example, from the rough ER to the Golgi apparatus, or from the Golgi apparatus to the outside of the cell.
Virus	Disease-causing particle. Not usually classed as a living organism.
Water potential	A measure of the tendency of a solution/cell to absorb water by osmosis.

Index

accuracy 45
actin 6
activation energy 8
active immunity 39
active transport 21, 24
AIDS 4, 29
alveoli 27–8, 30
amino acids 5, 6–7
amylases 13, 14–15
amylopectin 13–14
amylose 13–14
aneurysm 34
angina 34
antagonistic effects 33
antibodies 6, 37, 39
  monoclonal 40
antigens 37, 39
  purified 40
antihistamines 30
antisera 39–40
arteriosclerosis 34
assimilation 5
asthma 27, 30
atheroma 33–5
atherosclerosis 34–5
atria 31–3
atrial systole 31–2
atrioventricular (AV) valves 31–2
atrioventricular node 32

B lymphocytes (B cells) 37–8, 39
bacterial disease 25–6
baroreceptor cells 33
Benedict's solution 15
bile 6
binary fission 25
Biuret solution 8
blood clotting 6
breathing 28–9, 30
bronchioles 27–8
bronchodilators 30
brush border hydrolase enzymes 15
bundle of His 32

carbohydrates 5
  biochemical tests 15–16

digestion 12–15
carbon dioxide 33
carboxylic acids *see* organic acids
carcinogens 47–8
cardiac cycle 31–3
cardiovascular centre 33
cardiovascular disease 33–5
carrier proteins 22
catalysts 8
cell
  cytoplasm 16–17
  fractionation 17
  membranes 16, 18, 20–1, 42
  nucleus 16, 18
  organelles 16, 18–19
  typical 16–19
  ultracentrifugation 17
cell-mediated immunity 37–8
cells
  B lymphocytes (B cells) 37–8, 39
  chemoreceptor 33
  epithelial 6, 16
  eukaryotic 17–19, 25
  plasma 38
  prokarytic 25
  recognition 6
  red blood 38
  transport 6
  white blood 36, 38
cellulose 12, 13
chemoreceptor cells 33
cholera 4, 25–6
cholesterol 35
circulation
  pulmonary 30–1
  systemic 30–1
co-transport 22, 24
collagen 6, 7
communicable diseases *see*
  infectious diseases
condensation reaction 6
control experiments 43–4
controlled variables 43, 44
correlations 46, 47
cristae 18
cytoplasm 16, 18–19, 36

dead microorganisms 40
defensive functions 36–40
denaturation 8, 9–10
dependent variables 43
designing investigations 43–4
diaphragm 27–8
diastole 31–2
diffusion 22
digestive system 4–6
dipeptides 6–7
disaccharides 12, 13
disulphide bridges 8
DNA 18
double-blind investigations 48
drug resistance 29
drug trials 48

embolism 34
emphysema 4, 30
endocytosis 21
endoplasmic reticulum 18
endothelium 34
enzymes 6, 7
    active site 9
    brush border hydrolase 15
    enzyme-substrate complex 8, 10
    inhibitors 11–12
    and pH 10
    and temperature 9–10
epidemiology 47–8
epithelial cells 6, 16
erythrocytes 38
ester bonds 19–20
eukaryotic cells 17–19, 25
exocytosis 21, 36
exotoxins 4
experimentation 41–4
    accuracy and limitations 45
    associations and correlations 45–6
    on humans 46–8
extracellular digestion 25

facilitated diffusion 21, 22
fatty acids 5, 19–20
fibrosis 4, 29
fibrous proteins 7
flu vaccines 40
fluid mosaic model 21, 42
fructose 12, 24

galactose 12, 24
gastric juice 6
genetic diseases 4
globular proteins 7
glucose 5, 12, 13, 14, 24
    glycocidic bond 13, 19
glycerol 5, 19–20
glycogen 12, 13
Golgi apparatus 16, 19

haemoglobin 8
heart
    diseases 4, 33–5
    function 31–3
    structure 30–1
heartbeat 33
high blood pressure see hypertension
histones 18
homogenisation 17
hormones 12
human
    clinical trials 48
    experimentation subjects 26, 46–7
humoral immunity 37–8
hydrogen bonds 8
hydrolysis 4–5
hydrophilic groups 20
hydrophobic groups 20
hypertension 35
hypertonic solutions 23
hypotheses 9, 41–3
hypotonic solutions 23

immunisation 40
immunity 39–40
independent variables 43
induced fit hypothesis 9
infectious diseases 4
influenza 4, 40
informed consent 26
inhibitors
    competitive 11
    non-competitive 11–12
    reversible 11
insulin 8
intercostal muscles 27–8
interfaces 4
ion channels 22
isotonic buffer solution 17
isotonic solutions 23

keratin 6, 7

lactase 15
lactose 12, 13
lactose intolerance 15
latent diseases 30
leucocytes 38
lifestyle diseases 4
limitations 45
lipids 5, 19–20
   emulsion test 20
lipoproteins 35
   high density (HDLs) 35
   low density (LDLs) 35
live, attenuated vaccines 40
lock and key hypothesis 9
lungs
   diseases 29–30
   function 28–9
   structure 27
lysosomes 16, 19, 36
lysozyme 7

maltase 15
maltose 12, 13
medulla 28, 33
membranes
   partially permeable 22–3
   plasma 18, 21, 42
memory cells 38, 39
metabolism 4, 8, 12
micrographs 16
microvilli 16, 18, 24
mitochondrion 16, 18, 24
monoclonal antibodies (MABS) 40
monosaccharides 12–13
   α glucose 13
   β glucose 13
myocardial infarction 34
myocardium 34
myogenic muscle 33
myosin 6

neutrophils 36
non-communicable diseases *see* lifestyle diseases
non-reducing sugars 15

observation 41, 46
opportunistic infection 29
oral rehydration solutions (ORS) 26–7

organic acids 19–20
osmoregulation 24
osmosis 22–4

pancreatic juice 6
partially permeable membranes 22–3
passive immunity 39–40
pathogens 4, 25, 37–9, 40
peer review 42
phagocytosis 35
phospholipids 20
   bilayer 20–1
placebos 48
plasma cells 38
plasma membranes 18, 21, 42
polymers 12, 19
polypeptides 5–6, 7–8
polysaccharides 13–14
polyunsaturated fatty acids 19
primary immune response 38–9
prokarytic cells 25
proteins 5, 6–8
   primary structure 7
   secondary structure 7
      α helix 7
      β pleated sheet 7
   tertiary structure 8
      disulphide bridges 8
      hydrogen bonds 8
   quaternary structure 8
pulmonary circulation 30–1
Purkinje fibres 32

red blood cells 38
reducing sugars 15
rehydration therapy 26
reliability 44, 45
replicates 44
respiratory centre 28
ribosome 16, 19
Ringer's solution 23
rough endoplasmic reticulum 16, 18

saliva 6, 14
saturated fatty acids 19–20
scar tissue 29, 30
scientific research 41–8
secondary immune response 38–9
secondary infections 29
semilunar valves 31–2

simple squamous epithelium 28
sino-atrial node (SAN) 32
size and scaling 17
smoking 35, 47–8
smooth endoplasmic reticulum 16, 18
specific immune system 37–8
specific receptor sites 21
starch 12, 13–14, 15–16
steroids 30
substrates 8–9
    concentration 11
sucrase 8, 15
sucrose 12, 13
sugars 5, 12, 15
supernatant 17
systemic circulation 30–1

thermophilic bacteria 10
thermostable enzymes 10
thrombosis 34
trachea 27–8

trial guidlines 26–7
triglycerides 19–20
tubercles 30
tuberculosis (TB) 4, 29–30
turnover number 9

ultrastructure 17
unsaturated fatty acids 19–20

vaccination 40
vaccines 40
valid conclusions 44
variable factors 43
ventilation 28–9
ventricles 31–3
ventricular systole 31–2
vesicles 16, 19, 36
viruses 4

water potential 17, 23
white blood cells 36, 38

Notes

Notes

Notes